Family Meals

Family Meals

Elizabeth Seldon

Sundial

Contents

First published in 1977 by Sundial Books Limited
59 Grosvenor Street, London W1

Eighth impression, 1980

© 1977 Hennerwood Publications Limited
ISBN 0 904230 45 7

Printed in England by Severn Valley Press Limited

Introduction

The recipes in this book have been designed to help today's busy housewife or working wife produce appealing, nutritious dishes for the family. Its aim is to minimize the preparation time for meals by combining fresh foods and some convenience foods, particularly when they cost less than fresh produce. However, the dishes still maintain a home-made flavour and appearance.

Seasoning is one of the most important ingredients in a recipe and is so often omitted altogether or used too sparingly. Do remember to include it and use freshly-ground pepper which has more flavour than ready-ground pepper. Take care, though, when adding salt if bought stock cubes are being used, as some makes are on the salty side.

Herbs and spices do much to improve the flavour of food. Fresh herbs are the best to use, so it is well worth growing your own, either in a window box or in the garden, preferably near the kitchen door. Dried herbs once opened should be used within 6–8 months of purchase. If fresh herbs have been specified in a recipe and only dried herbs are available, it is best to use half the quantity mentioned as dried herbs are more concentrated.

It is almost as important for food to look attractive as to have good flavour. It is worth therefore spending a few extra minutes choosing a suitable plate or dish for serving and add a dash of colour – some chopped parsley or chives, lemon wedges or a few tomato slices. These make all the difference to an otherwise ordinary looking meal.

Nutritionally well balanced meals are essential for good health so it is necessary to know a little about the food we eat so that you can plan meals to provide these vital nutrients.

There are six main food groups, namely proteins, fats, carbohydrates, minerals, vitamins and water. Each group has its own particular function. Proteins, which build new tissues and replace old ones, can either be animal or vegetable. Animal proteins tend to be the expensive items on the food bill; meat, fish, poultry, cheese, eggs and milk, but are higher in food value than their vegetable counterparts. These include peas, beans, lentils and nuts. To get best protein value, though, choose food from both sources.

Fats, which provide warmth and long term energy are found in butter, margarine, vegetable fats and oils, fish oils, meats, cream cheeses, cream, bacon, eggs and thick cream milk.

Carbohydrates, which provide energy and supply about half our calorie intake, are present in flour, cereals, bread, potatoes, rice, sugar, jam, biscuits, cakes. These should be used in the diet with care as they are fattening foods.

Minerals regulate body functions – there are many present in foods but there are a few main ones. Firstly, iron, found in liver, kidney, heart, eggs, whole grain cereals and to a lesser extent meat, fish, green vegetables and potatoes. This mineral forms the red blood cells which carry oxygen around the body. Secondly, calcium and phosphorus form most of the hard structure of bones and teeth so are very important in children's diets and for pregnant mothers. All adults require calcium but in smaller amounts. Cheese, milk, eggs, sardines, bread, and celery provide us with these minerals. Sodium is another important mineral as it is present in body fluids in the form of salt. In hot climates extra salt may be needed in the diet.

Vitamins are substances required in very small quantities for protection against illness and for general good health. All vitamins can normally be obtained in a good mixed diet of natural foods, particularly fresh fruit and vegetables, liver, kidney, meat, fish and eggs.

Water is also vital to health and we need to drink at least $1\frac{3}{4}$ litres (3 pints) a day – coffee, tea, etc., can be counted here. Lastly, roughage, an essential constituent in the diet. This is vital for getting rid of waste matter, but our bodies cannot digest it. It is found in whole grain cereals, bran, wholemeal bread, fresh fruit and vegetables and some should be eaten daily. So, balanced meals constitute foods from all the food groups.

It would be very tedious to work out nutrients for each meal, therefore it is best to plan a daily meal pattern with average requirements to meet body needs.

Being overweight is a common problem today, and is seldom due to glandular trouble but more likely to bad eating habits. It is best to tackle the trouble as early as possible both in children and adults. The usual cause is from eating a high proportion of carbohydrates and fats; and eating snacks between meals, so these must be checked. Losing weight must be achieved slowly and crash diets avoided at all costs.

Many people leave meal planning until an hour or so before the meal but it is much more economical and gives better nutritional balance if you plan for the week ahead. Naturally the time of year and the weather influence the menu but don't be too rigid – salads for example can be enjoyed all the year round. Always buy foods in season.

By planning a week's menus in advance your shopping expeditions can be reduced as well as the time you spend in the kitchen. An example of forward planning is to make a large beef casserole which is then divided into three different dishes and stored in the refrigerator or freezer so that no dish is ever re-heated twice. Again a lamb stew can be divided into two, one being flavoured with tomatoes and herbs, and the other with root vegetables. When buying a joint, buy

one large enough to last for a hot and a cold meal, and use the leftovers to stuff pancakes or omelettes.

Fresh vegetables provide a crunchy texture, delicious flavour and good nutritive value, so are well worth the preparation. In any meal don't include pastry in more than one course; and if you are serving a soup there is no need for a pudding – fresh fruit is a refreshing alternative, not too filling and good for all the family. If the family are still hungry after their pudding serve some cheese to round off the meal and fill them up. For hungry teenagers who are not overweight, include more of the filling foods like pasta, potatoes, rice and pastry toppings, to go with the main course.

As we spend a quarter to a third of our income on food it is well worth using time planning meals and shopping economically. Money saving meals don't need to be mundane – a little thought will produce interesting and exciting dishes.

Oxtail soup

Metric	Imperial
25g margarine	1oz margarine
1 oxtail, jointed and trimmed of excess fat	1 oxtail, jointed and trimmed of excess fat
2 onions, peeled and sliced	2 onions, peeled and sliced
2 carrots, peeled and chopped	2 carrots, peeled and chopped
2 sticks celery, scrubbed and chopped	2 sticks celery, scrubbed and chopped
2 rashers lean bacon, rinded and chopped	2 rashers lean bacon, rinded and chopped
½ teaspoon dried thyme	½ teaspoon dried thyme
Parsley stalks	Parsley stalks
1 × 15ml spoon pearl barley	1 tablespoon pearl barley
1¾l water	3 pints water
Salt and black pepper	Salt and black pepper
1 × 15ml spoon sherry	1 tablespoon sherry
2 × 5ml spoons tomato purée	2 teaspoons tomato purée
50g flour	2oz flour
Cold water	Cold water
To finish:	To finish:
Chopped parsley	Chopped parsley
Small squares of toast	Small squares of toast

Cooking Time: 3½ hours

This soup is almost a meal in itself. Heat the margarine and fry the pieces of oxtail until lightly browned. Drain off excess fat and stir vegetables, bacon, herbs and barley in with meat. Pour on cold water and bring to the boil. Season with salt and pepper. Reduce heat and simmer covered for about 3 hours until meat falls away from the bone. Skim off excess fat and return stock to pan. Remove meat from oxtail pieces and return this to pan with sherry and tomato purée. Blend flour with cold water. Pour some stock onto blended flour and return all to the pan. Bring to the boil stirring and simmer for a further 5 minutes. Taste and adjust seasoning. Garnish with plenty of chopped parsley and serve with small squares of toast.

Minestrone soup

Metric	Imperial
75g butter beans	3 oz butter beans
25g margarine	1oz margarine
1 medium-sized onion, peeled and sliced	1 medium-sized onion, peeled and sliced
1 carrot, peeled and diced	1 carrot, peeled and diced
2 sticks celery, scrubbed and chopped	2 sticks celery, scrubbed and chopped
1 rasher streaky bacon, rinded and chopped	1 rasher streaky bacon, rinded and chopped
1 bouquet garni	1 bouquet garni
1½l beef stock	2½ pints beef stock
Salt and freshly ground black pepper	Salt and freshly ground black pepper
1 leek, cleaned and sliced	1 leek, cleaned and sliced
2 tomatoes, peeled and quartered	2 tomatoes, peeled and quartered
25g frozen peas	1oz frozen peas
25g pasta shells	1oz pasta shells
To finish:	To finish:
Parmesan cheese	Parmesan cheese

Cooking Time: 1¾ hours

Soak the beans overnight in water. Drain well. Heat margarine and lightly fry the onion, carrot, celery and bacon. Add the beans and bouquet garni and pour the stock over the vegetables. Bring slowly to the boil, season and simmer for about 1 hour in a covered pan. Add the leeks, tomatoes, peas and pasta shells, and simmer for a further 30 minutes. Taste and adjust seasoning and serve with grated Parmesan cheese.

Oxtail soup; Minestrone soup; Chicken broth

Chicken broth

Metric

1 chicken carcass, halved
1¾l water
1 large onion, peeled and
sliced
1 carrot, peeled and diced
1 stick celery, scrubbed
and chopped
Salt and freshly ground
black pepper
1 bay leaf
25g long grain rice

To finish:
2 × 15ml spoons finely
chopped parsley

Imperial

1 chicken carcass, halved
3 pints water
1 large onion, peeled and
sliced
1 carrot, peeled and diced
1 stick celery, scrubbed
and chopped
Salt and freshly ground
black pepper
1 bay leaf
1oz long grain rice

To finish:
2 tablespoons finely
chopped parsley

Cooking Time: 1 hour 40 minutes

This is an excellent way of making a tasty, warming and inexpensive soup. Alternatively the strained liquid may be used as chicken stock, required in many recipes. Put the carcass into a large pan and cover with water. Add vegetables, seasoning and bay leaf. Bring to the boil and simmer for about 1¼ hours. Remove any excess fat from the surface with a spoon, add the rice and simmer for about 15 minutes. Taste and adjust seasoning. Remove carcass, pour into tureen and garnish with chopped parsley. A game bird or turkey carcass can be used to make this broth.

Cream of carrot soup

Metric	Imperial
25g butter	1oz butter
450g carrots, peeled and chopped	1lb carrots, peeled and chopped
1 stick celery, scrubbed and chopped	1 stick celery, scrubbed and chopped
1 small onion, peeled and sliced	1 small onion, peeled and sliced
¼ turnip, peeled and diced	¼ turnip, peeled and diced
1 rasher streaky bacon, rinded and chopped	1 rasher streaky bacon, rinded and chopped
1 × 15ml spoon flour	1 tablespoon flour
1¼l chicken stock	2 pints chicken stock
Salt and freshly ground black pepper	Salt and freshly ground black pepper

To finish:
Watercress leaves

To finish:
Watercress leaves

Cooking Time: 45 minutes

Heat butter in a large pan and fry the vegetables and bacon for about 5 minutes. Add the flour and cook for a minute. Gradually stir in the stock, bring to the boil. Season well and allow to simmer covered for 30–40 minutes until vegetables are soft. Allow to cool, purée to a cream in an electric blender or pass through a sieve. Return to the pan, re-heat, taste and adjust seasoning, garnish with cress and serve with French bread.

Cream of celery soup

Metric	Imperial
15g butter	½oz butter
1 head of celery, scrubbed and chopped	1 head of celery, scrubbed and chopped
1 × 15ml spoon flour	1 tablespoon flour
750ml well-flavoured chicken stock	1¼ pints well-flavoured chicken stock
Salt and freshly ground black pepper	Salt and freshly ground black pepper
Bouquet garni	Bouquet garni

To finish:
Croûtons

To finish:
Croûtons

Cooking Time: 35 minutes

Heat the butter and fry the celery gently for 5 minutes. Stir in the flour and cook for 2 minutes. Add the stock and bring to the boil, stirring all the time. Season well, add the bouquet garni, cover the pan and simmer for about 30 minutes. Remove the bouquet garni and sieve or purée half the soup in an electric blender (thus retaining some pieces of celery), mix and return to the pan. Re-heat, taste and adjust seasoning. Serve garnished with croûtons.

Cream of watercress soup

Metric	Imperial
50g butter	2oz butter
1 onion, peeled and sliced	1 onion, peeled and sliced
2 bunches watercress, washed, stalks removed and roughly chopped	2 bunches watercress, washed, stalks removed and roughly chopped
450ml chicken stock	¾ pint chicken stock
25g flour	1oz flour
300ml milk	½ pint milk
Salt and freshly ground black pepper	Salt and freshly ground black pepper
1 × 15ml spoon cream (optional)	1 tablespoon cream (optional)

To finish:
Watercress leaves
Croûtons, optional

To finish:
Watercress leaves
Croûtons, optional

Cooking Time: 45 minutes

Heat half the butter and fry onion until soft. Stir in the prepared watercress and cook a further few minutes. Pour in the stock, cover and simmer for 20 minutes. Allow to cool slightly. In another pan heat the rest of the butter and stir in flour. Cook for a few minutes and off the heat blend in the milk gradually. Return to the hob and bring sauce to the boil, stirring all the time. Season and pour into the watercress and stock. Transfer to an electric blender and purée to a smooth cream. Taste and adjust seasoning. Return to the pan and re-heat adding cream if liked. Serve garnished with a few whole watercress leaves and croûtons.

Cream of carrot soup; Cream of celery soup; Cream of watercress soup; French onion soup

French onion soup

Metric

65g butter
700g onions, peeled and sliced
1 clove of garlic, peeled and crushed (optional)
1 × 15ml spoon flour
1¼l well-flavoured beef stock
Salt and freshly ground black pepper

To finish:
4 slices French bread, toasted
50g Cheddar cheese, grated

Imperial

2½oz butter
1½lb onions, peeled and sliced
1 clove of garlic, peeled and crushed (optional)
1 tablespoon flour
2 pints well-flavoured beef stock
Salt and freshly ground black pepper

To finish:
4 slices French bread, toasted
2oz Cheddar cheese, grated

Cooking Time: 25 minutes

Heat the butter in a pan, and when foaming add the onions. Fry gently until soft and golden brown. Add the crushed garlic, stir in the flour and cook for a couple of minutes. Allow to cool slightly before adding the stock. Bring to the boil stirring constantly. Season well, reduce the heat, cover and allow to simmer for 20 minutes. Taste and adjust seasoning.

To finish: Top 4 slices of toasted French bread with grated cheese and place under a preheated grill until cheese melts and bubbles. Pour the soup into individual warmed bowls and float a slice of toasted cheese on each. Serve immediately.

Mushroom soup

Metric	Imperial
25g butter	1oz butter
1 small onion, peeled and sliced	1 small onion, peeled and sliced
225g button mushrooms, washed and sliced	8oz button mushrooms, washed and sliced
25g flour	1oz flour
600ml well-flavoured chicken stock	1 pint well-flavoured chicken stock
150ml milk	¼ pint milk
Salt and freshly ground black pepper	Salt and freshly ground black pepper

To finish:
Chopped parsley, optional

To finish:
Chopped parsley, optional

Cooking Time: 20 minutes

Heat the butter and fry the onion until soft. Add the mushrooms and sauté for about 5 minutes. Stir in the flour and cook for 2 minutes. Allow to cool slightly, then add the stock and milk gradually. Bring to the boil stirring all the time. Season well, cover and simmer gently for about 20 minutes. Serve hot, garnished with chopped parsley if liked.

Fresh tomato soup

Metric	Imperial
40g butter for frying	1½oz butter for frying
1 small onion, peeled and sliced	1 small onion, peeled and sliced
1 rasher streaky bacon, rinded and chopped	1 rasher streaky bacon, rinded and chopped
1 stick celery, scrubbed and chopped	1 stick celery, scrubbed and chopped
¾kg tomatoes, skinned and roughly chopped	1½lb tomatoes, skinned and roughly chopped
2 × 15ml spoons flour	2 tablespoons flour
600ml chicken stock	1 pint chicken stock
1 × 5ml spoon dried basil	1 teaspoon dried basil
Salt and freshly ground black pepper	Salt and freshly ground black pepper
4 × 5ml spoon tomato purée (optional)	4 teaspoons tomato purée (optional)
1 × 15ml spoon medium dry sherry	1 tablespoon medium dry sherry

To finish:
Chopped parsley

To finish:
Chopped parsley

Cooking Time: 40 minutes

Heat the butter in a pan and fry the onion, bacon and celery until soft but not coloured. Add the tomatoes and cook for a few minutes. Stir in the flour, add the stock, basil, seasoning and tomato purée and bring slowly to the boil. Simmer for 30 minutes. Pass soup through a sieve, or purée in an electric blender. Return to the pan, add sherry, re-heat, taste and adjust seasoning, and serve sprinkled with chopped parsley.

Leek and potato soup

Metric	Imperial
25g butter	1oz butter
450g leeks, well cleaned and sliced	1lb leeks, well cleaned and sliced
1 small onion, peeled and sliced	1 small onion, peeled and sliced
2 medium-sized potatoes, peeled and sliced	2 medium-sized potatoes, peeled and sliced
1l chicken stock	1¾ pints chicken stock
Salt and freshly ground black pepper	Salt and freshly ground black pepper

To finish:
Chopped chives

To finish:
Chopped chives

Cooking Time: 40 minutes

Heat the butter in a large saucepan and fry the vegetables for about 5 minutes until soft. Add the stock and seasoning, bring to the boil and simmer covered, for 30 minutes, until the potatoes are soft. Sieve the soup or purée in a blender, and return to the pan. Re-heat, taste and adjust seasoning. Serve garnished with chopped chives.

Mushroom soup; Fresh tomato soup; Leek and potato soup; Cream of artichoke soup

Cream of artichoke soup

Metric

40g butter
1 large onion, peeled and
sliced
¾kg Jerusalem artichokes,
peeled and sliced
300ml milk
600ml chicken stock
Salt and freshly ground
black pepper

To finish:
Sprigs watercress

Imperial

1½oz butter
1 large onion, peeled and
sliced
1½lb Jerusalem artichokes,
peeled and sliced
½ pint milk
1 pint chicken stock
Salt and freshly ground
black pepper

To finish:
Sprigs watercress

Cooking Time: 30 minutes

This is a deliciously flavoured soup and is well worth making when Jerusalem artichokes are in season from November to June. Heat butter in a pan and cook onion until soft but not coloured. Add the artichokes to the pan, pour over the milk and cook slowly for about 7 minutes, shaking the pan occasionally. Pour the stock into the pan, season, cover and simmer for about 20 minutes. Allow to cool, then purée to a cream in an electric blender or pass through a sieve. Return to the pan, taste and adjust seasoning, re-heat and serve garnished with sprigs of watercress.

Cheese crust vegetable pie

Metric	Imperial
For the cheese pastry:	For the cheese pastry:
150g flour	*6oz flour*
Pinch of salt	*Pinch of salt*
100g margarine	*4oz margarine*
75g Cheddar cheese, finely grated	*3oz Cheddar cheese, finely grated*
2–3 × 15ml spoons cold water, to mix	*2–3 tablespoons cold water, to mix*
For the filling:	For the filling:
50g butter	*2oz butter*
1 onion, peeled and sliced	*1 onion, peeled and sliced*
3 carrots, peeled and sliced	*3 carrots, peeled and sliced*
198g can corn kernels	*7oz can corn kernels*
50g mushrooms, washed and sliced	*2oz mushrooms, washed and sliced*
2 sticks celery, scrubbed and chopped	*2 sticks celery, scrubbed and chopped*
50g packet leek soup	*2oz packet leek soup*
Freshly ground black pepper	*Freshly ground black pepper*
1 egg, beaten, to glaze	*1 egg, beaten, to glaze*

Cooking Time: 55 minutes
Oven: 200°C, 400°F, Gas Mark 6
180°C, 350°F, Gas Mark 4

Packet soups are ideal as sauce substitutes in pies and casseroles. The addition of a leek soup here provides a delicious flavouring. Sift the flour and salt into a mixing bowl. Rub fat into flour and stir in cheese. Bind together with water. Wrap in foil and leave in a cool place until needed. Heat butter in a pan and fry vegetables for a few minutes. Drain well on kitchen paper. Make up packet of leek soup as directed on the packet, but using 600ml (1 pint) water only. Stir vegetables into leek soup, season with pepper and pour into a 750ml (1½ pint) pie dish. Roll out pastry to top the pie. Trim and flute edges. Use left-over pastry to make leaves to decorate pie top. Brush pastry with beaten egg and cook in a hot oven for 15 minutes, then reduce heat for a further 40 minutes. Serve hot with buttered noodles.

Stuffed aubergines

Metric	Imperial
3 medium-sized aubergines, washed and stalks removed	*3 medium-sized aubergines, washed and stalks removed*
Salt	*Salt*
25g butter	*1oz butter*
1 medium-sized onion, peeled and finely chopped	*1 medium-sized onion, peeled and finely chopped*
175g minced beef	*6oz minced beef*
1 clove garlic, peeled and crushed	*1 clove garlic, peeled and crushed*
1 × 15ml spoon finely chopped parsley	*1 tablespoon finely chopped parsley*
396g can tomatoes	*14oz can tomatoes*
2 × 5ml spoons tomato paste	*2 teaspoons tomato paste*
1 × 5ml spoon dried marjoram	*1 teaspoon dried marjoram*
Freshly ground black pepper	*Freshly ground black pepper*
2 × 5ml spoons cornflour	*2 teaspoons cornflour*
100g Cheddar cheese, coarsely grated	*4oz Cheddar cheese, coarsely grated*

Cooking Time: 30 minutes
Oven: 180°C, 350°F, Gas Mark 4

Slice the aubergines in half lengthwise. Scoop out the flesh carefully and chop finely. Put flesh on a large plate, sprinkle with salt and leave for 30 minutes. Blanch aubergine skins in boiling water for 5 minutes. Remove and place on a serving dish. Heat butter, and cook onion until soft. Stir in minced beef and cook until brown, stirring frequently. Add garlic, parsley, tomatoes, paste and herbs. Season with black pepper. Bring to boil. Blend cornflour with a little cold water and add to beef tomato sauce. Return to the boil, then remove from the heat. Drain aubergine flesh in a sieve and rinse in cold water. Stir half the flesh into the beef and tomato mixture, and use to stuff the aubergine halves. Top each one with grated cheese and cook in a moderate oven for about 30 minutes. Serve hot with a tossed green salad. Use remaining aubergine flesh in a Bolognese sauce or as a vegetable in cheese sauce.
Serves 6 as a starter

Courgettes with herbs

Metric	Imperial	Cooking Time: 5 minutes
¾kg courgettes, washed, topped, tailed and quartered lengthwise	1½lb courgettes, washed, topped, tailed and quartered lengthwise	Cook courgettes in boiling, salted water for 5 minutes. Drain and toss in butter. Add plenty of freshly ground black pepper and chopped tarragon.
25g butter	1oz butter	
Freshly ground black pepper	Freshly ground black pepper	
Chopped tarragon	Chopped tarragon	

Buttered celeriac

Metric	Imperial	Cooking Time: 20 minutes
¾kg celeriac, leaves and root fibres removed	1½lb celeriac, leaves and root fibres removed	Cook celeriac in boiling, salted water for about 20 minutes. Drain, peel and slice. Toss in butter and add salt, pepper and chopped parsley. This can be served coated in a cheese sauce. (See recipe for Cauliflower au Gratin, page 20.)
25g butter	1oz butter	
Salt and freshly ground black pepper	Salt and freshly ground black pepper	
Chopped parsley	Chopped parsley	

Runner beans with carrots

Metric	Imperial	Cooking Time: 30 minutes
225g young carrots, scraped and sliced	8oz young carrots, scraped and sliced	Put carrots in a pan and pour over enough water to cover the vegetables. Season, cover and cook for 10 minutes. Add the beans and oil. Sprinkle with thyme, cover and cook a further 20 minutes.
Salt and freshly ground black pepper	Salt and freshly ground black pepper	
450g runner beans, stringed and thinly sliced	1lb runner beans, stringed and thinly sliced	
2 × 15ml spoons oil	2 tablespoons oil	
½ teaspoon dried thyme	½ teaspoon dried thyme	

Corn on the cob parcels

Metric	Imperial	Cooking Time: 15 minutes
		Oven: 160°C, 325°F, Gas Mark 3
4 fresh corn cobs, husks and silks removed or frozen corn cobs	4 fresh corn cobs, husks and silks removed or frozen corn cobs	Cook corn in boiling water for 5 minutes. Drain and place each in a piece of buttered foil. Melt butter, add herbs and pour a little over each corn. Season well, cover with the foil and bake on a baking sheet in a slow oven for 10 minutes.
50g butter	2oz butter	
1 × 15ml spoon fresh thyme	1 tablespoon fresh thyme	
Salt and freshly ground black pepper	Salt and freshly ground black pepper	

Leeks

Metric	Imperial	
¾kg fresh leeks, well-washed, trimmed and halved	*1½lb fresh leeks, well-washed, trimmed and halved*	Cooking Time: 10 minutes

Butter
Freshly ground black pepper

Butter
Freshly ground black pepper

Cook prepared leeks in boiling, salted water for about 10 minutes. Drain thoroughly and toss in butter. Add plenty of freshly ground black pepper. Cooked leeks can be served cold in a French dressing, see page 29.

Glazed carrots

Metric

Imperial

Cooking Time: approx. 15 minutes

50g butter
450g young carrots, scraped and quartered lengthwise
Salt and freshly ground black pepper
Pinch of sugar

To finish:
Knob of butter
Chopped parsley

2oz butter
1lb young carrots, scraped and quartered lengthwise
Salt and freshly ground black pepper
Pinch of sugar

To finish:
Knob of butter
Chopped parsley

Melt the butter in a pan. Add the carrots, seasoning, sugar and just enough water to cover the vegetables. Cook slowly without a lid until the carrots are soft and the water evaporated, leaving carrots with a slight glaze. Add a knob of butter and sprinkle liberally with chopped parsley.

Roast parsnips

Metric

Imperial

Cooking Time: 50 minutes

¾kg parsnips, peeled, quartered and sliced

To finish:
Chopped parsley

1½lb parsnips, peeled, quartered and sliced

To finish:
Chopped parsley

Cook prepared parsnips in boiling, salted water for 5 minutes. Drain well. Place in the fat around the joint and cook for about ¾ hour. Garnish with chopped parsley.

Creamed spinach

Metric

Imperial

Cooking Time: 20–25 minutes

1½kg fresh spinach, washed several times and coarse stalks removed
25–50g butter
3 × 15ml spoons single cream
Salt and freshly ground black pepper
Pinch powdered nutmeg

3lb fresh spinach, washed several times and coarse stalks removed
1–2oz butter
3 tablespoons single cream
Salt and freshly ground black pepper
Pinch powdered nutmeg

Pack washed spinach in a saucepan. Heat gently turning the spinach occasionally. Bring to the boil and cook for 10–15 minutes until soft. Drain thoroughly and pass through a sieve. Add butter, cream, salt and freshly ground black pepper and nutmeg to the purée. Return to the pan and re-heat.

Leeks; Glazed carrots; Roast parsnips; Creamed spinach

VEGETABLES

Cauliflower au gratin

Metric	Imperial
1 cauliflower, washed and trimmed	1 cauliflower, washed and trimmed
25g butter	1oz butter
25g flour	1oz flour
300ml milk	½ pint milk
100g Cheddar cheese, finely grated	4oz Cheddar cheese, finely grated
Salt and freshly ground black pepper	Salt and freshly ground black pepper
25g fresh white breadcrumbs	1oz fresh white breadcrumbs

Cooking Time: 25–30 minutes

Cook the cauliflower in boiling, salted water for 10 minutes. Drain and place in an ovenproof dish. Melt the butter, add the flour and cook for a few minutes. Allow to cool slightly before adding the milk gradually. Bring to the boil. Stir in 75g (3oz) grated cheese, and season well. Pour over the cauliflower. Mix the remaining cheese and breadcrumbs together and sprinkle over the cauliflower. Brown under a hot grill. Serve with bacon rolls.

Stuffed mushrooms

Metric	Imperial
4 large fresh mushrooms, wiped clean	4 large fresh mushrooms, wiped clean
15g butter	½oz butter
1 rasher streaky bacon, rinded and chopped	1 rasher streaky bacon, rinded and chopped
20g fresh white breadcrumbs	¾oz fresh white breadcrumbs
2 × 5ml spoons chopped parsley	2 teaspoons chopped parsley
Grated rind of ¼ lemon	Grated rind of ¼ lemon
½ teaspoon lemon juice	½ teaspoon lemon juice
50g Cheddar cheese, finely grated	2oz Cheddar cheese, finely grated
Salt and freshly ground black pepper	Salt and freshly ground black pepper
To finish:	To finish:
Watercress	Watercress

Cooking Time: 15–20 minutes
Oven: 170°C, 325°F, Gas Mark 3

Remove stalks from mushrooms and chop finely. Heat butter and fry mushroom stalks and bacon for a few minutes. Off the heat stir in breadcrumbs, parsley, lemon rind and juice and cheese. Season well. Place mushroom caps on a greased baking sheet, divide filling between each one and bake for 15–20 minutes in a slow oven. Garnish with sprigs of watercress and serve hot as a starter, or an accompaniment to pork or lamb.

Stuffed tomatoes

Metric	Imperial
4 large tomatoes, washed	4 large tomatoes, washed
25g butter	1oz butter
100g button mushrooms, washed and finely chopped	4oz button mushrooms, washed and finely chopped
2 shallots, washed, roots removed, peeled and finely chopped	2 shallots, washed, roots removed, peeled and finely chopped
2 × 15ml spoons fresh white breadcrumbs	2 tablespoons fresh white breadcrumbs
2 × 5ml spoons mixed dried herbs	2 teaspoons mixed dried herbs
Salt and freshly ground black pepper	Salt and freshly ground black pepper
1 × 15ml spoon cheese, finely grated	1 tablespoon cheese, finely grated

Cooking Time: 15 minutes
Oven: 190°C, 375°F, Gas Mark 5

Slice the tops off each tomato. Carefully scoop out the seeds. Heat butter in a pan and cook mushrooms and shallots for a few minutes. Stir in the crumbs, herbs, seasoning and cheese. Fill the tomatoes and replace tops. Cook in a moderate oven for about 15 minutes.

Cauliflower au gratin; Stuffed mushrooms; Stuffed tomatoes

Potatoes

Peel potatoes as thinly as possible, preferably using a potato peeler. New potatoes are scraped or brushed. If prepared potatoes are not to be cooked immediately, cover with water to prevent discoloration.

Creamed: Mash drained, cooked potatoes with a little butter, salt, pepper and a little milk. Beat until fluffy. Spoon into a serving dish and decorate with a fork. Garnish with chopped parsley.

Jacket: Scrub even-sized old potatoes well, cut a cross through the skin on each potato and bake in a hot oven, 200°C, 400°F, Gas Mark 6 for 1–1¼ hours. Dot each with a knob of butter before serving.

Sauté: Boil potatoes until they are just cooked. Drain and slice thickly. Heat oil in a pan and fry until golden on both sides.

Baked Stuffed Potatoes: Cook as above for jacket potatoes, but prick potatoes all over instead of cutting a cross. When cooked, cut in half lengthwise and scoop out the centres, taking care to keep skins intact. Mash potato in a basin and add one of the following stuffings:

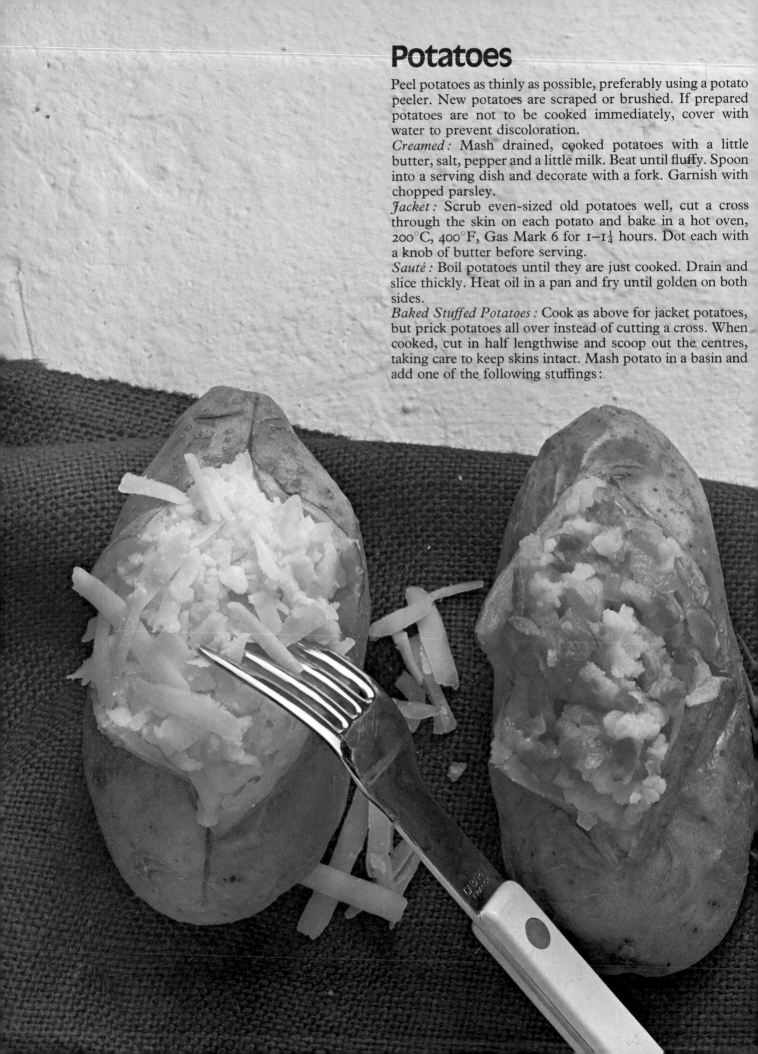

Fillings for baked potatoes

Metric
1) *75g Cheddar cheese,
   grated
   25g butter
   A little milk
   Salt and freshly
   ground black pepper*
2) *75g bacon, rinded,
   chopped and fried
   A little milk
   Salt and freshly ground
   black pepper*
3) *3 × 15ml spoons
   soured cream
   2 × 5ml spoons chives,
   washed and chopped*

Imperial
1) *3oz Cheddar cheese,
   grated
   1oz butter
   A little milk
   Salt and freshly ground
   black pepper*
2) *3oz bacon, rinded,
   chopped and fried
   A little milk
   Salt and freshly ground
   black pepper*
3) *3 tablespoons soured
   cream
   2 teaspoons chives,
   washed and chopped*

Baked potatoes with fillings

Potatoes normande

Metric	Imperial
40g butter	1½oz butter
¾kg potatoes, peeled and thinly sliced	1½lb potatoes, peeled and thinly sliced
Salt and freshly ground black pepper	Salt and freshly ground black pepper
300ml milk	½ pint milk

Cooking Time: 1–1½ hours
Oven: 180°C, 350°F, Gas Mark 4

A delicious way to cook potatoes to ring the changes. Use a little of the butter to grease a casserole dish. Layer the slices of potato in the dish and season well between each layer. Pour the milk over the potatoes, dot the remaining butter over the top slices and bake in a moderate oven for about 1–1½ hours until the potatoes are soft. Serve as an accompaniment to roast beef, pork and lamb.

Braised red cabbage

Metric	Imperial
50g butter	2oz butter
1 medium-sized onion, peeled and sliced	1 medium-sized onion, peeled and sliced
1 clove of garlic, peeled and crushed	1 clove of garlic, peeled and crushed
450g red cabbage, trimmed and shredded	1lb red cabbage, trimmed and shredded
1 cooking apple, peeled, cored and sliced	1 cooking apple, peeled, cored and sliced
3 × 15ml spoons white wine vinegar	3 tablespoons white wine vinegar
3 × 15ml spoons water	3 tablespoons water
25g sugar	1oz sugar
Salt and freshly ground black pepper	Salt and freshly ground black pepper

Cooking Time: 45 minutes
Oven: 180°C, 350°F, Gas Mark 4

Heat the butter in a saucepan and fry the onion and garlic for a few minutes. Add the cabbage and apples and cook for 5 minutes stirring with a wooden spoon. Spoon mixture into an ovenproof dish. Combine the vinegar and water, add the sugar and pour this over the cabbage. Season liberally, cover and cook in a moderate oven for about 45 minutes. Drain, or serve with a slotted spoon. This is a delicious accompaniment to pork and veal dishes.

Cheese topped bubble and squeak

Metric	Imperial
¾kg old potatoes, peeled	1½lb old potatoes, peeled
A little milk	A little milk
A knob of butter	A knob of butter
450g green cabbage, washed and chopped	1lb green cabbage, washed and chopped
1 small onion, peeled and finely chopped	1 small onion, peeled and finely chopped
Salt and freshly ground black pepper	Salt and freshly ground black pepper
75g Cheddar cheese, grated	3oz Cheddar cheese, grated

Cooking Time: 30–40 minutes
Oven: 200°C, 400°F, Gas Mark 6

Cook potatoes in salted water until soft. Drain and cream with a little milk and butter. Plunge cabbage into boiling, salted water and cook for 5 minutes. Drain and chop. Combine potato and cabbage with the chopped onion. Taste and adjust seasoning. Spoon into an oiled baking dish, top with the grated cheese and cook in a hot oven for about 30–40 minutes, until evenly browned. Serve hot cut into quarters.

Braised celery

Metric

25g butter
1 onion, peeled and finely
chopped
2 medium-sized carrots,
peeled and diced
8 sticks celery, scrubbed,
trimmed and cut in half
lengthwise
300ml chicken stock
Salt and freshly ground
black pepper

To finish:
Chopped parsley

Imperial

1oz butter
1 onion, peeled and finely
chopped
2 medium-sized carrots,
peeled and diced
8 sticks celery, scrubbed,
trimmed and cut in half
lengthwise
½ pint chicken stock
Salt and freshly ground
black pepper

To finish:
Chopped parsley

Cooking Time: 1–1¼ hours
Oven: 180°C, 350°F, Gas Mark 4

This is a useful way to cook celery as it bakes with the Sunday roast leaving more space on the hob. Heat butter and fry onion and carrots for a couple of minutes. Add celery and cook for 2 minutes. Put vegetables into an oven-proof dish and pour on stock. Season well. Cover and cook in a moderate oven for about 1 to 1¼ hours. Serve garnished with chopped parsley. This goes well with pork and duck.

Baked stuffed marrow

Metric

1 medium-sized marrow,
washed
100g packet savoury
tomato rice
25g margarine
1 onion, peeled and finely
chopped
2 rashers bacon, rinded
and finely chopped
350g minced beef
75g Cheddar cheese, finely
grated
Salt and freshly ground
black pepper
1 × 5ml spoon
Worcestershire sauce
1 small egg, beaten

To finish:
*Tomato sauce (see recipe
for Pork and Beef Loaf,
page 42)*

Imperial

1 medium-sized marrow,
washed
4oz packet savoury
tomato rice
1oz margarine
1 onion, peeled and finely
chopped
2 rashers bacon, rinded
and finely chopped
12 oz minced beef
3oz Cheddar cheese, finely
grated
Salt and freshly ground
black pepper
1 teaspoon Worcestershire
sauce
1 small egg, beaten

To finish:
*Tomato sauce (see recipe
for Pork and Beef Loaf,
page 42)*

Cooking Time: 45–60 minutes
Oven: 180°C, 350°F, Gas Mark 4

Slice off one end of the marrow, scoop out the seeds. Cook the savoury rice as directed on the packet. Heat margarine, fry onion and bacon for a few minutes. Stir in minced beef and brown meat well. Drain off excess fat, and stir in grated cheese and cooked rice. Season well and add Worcestershire sauce. Bind mixture with beaten egg. Fill marrow cavity with stuffing, wrap in oiled foil and place on a baking sheet. Bake in a moderate oven for about 45 to 60 minutes. Serve hot in slices with tomato sauce.

Cole slaw

Metric

450g raw white cabbage,
shredded
2 carrots, scraped and
grated
2 sticks celery, scrubbed
and chopped
1 small onion, peeled and
grated
25g sultanas
6 × 15ml spoons
mayonnaise
Salt and freshly ground
black pepper

Imperial

1lb raw white cabbage,
shredded
2 carrots, scraped and
grated
2 sticks celery, scrubbed
and chopped
1 small onion, peeled and
grated
1oz sultanas
6 tablespoons
mayonnaise
Salt and freshly ground
black pepper

Turn the cabbage into a bowl. Stir in the carrot, celery and onion. Add the sultanas and mix well together. Toss in mayonnaise and season salad with salt and black pepper. Garnish with sprigs of watercress. This salad will store well in the refrigerator for 2 days in a sealed plastic container.

To finish:
Watercress

To finish:
Watercress

Mushroom salad

Metric

Salt and freshly ground
black pepper
Pinch dry English
mustard
9 × 15ml spoons olive or
corn oil
3 × 15ml spoons wine
vinegar
1 × 15ml spoons finely
chopped parsley
1 clove of garlic, peeled
and crushed
350g button mushrooms,
washed and sliced

Imperial

Salt and freshly ground
black pepper
Pinch dry English
mustard
9 tablespoons olive or
corn oil
3 tablespoons wine
vinegar
1 tablespoon finely
chopped parsley
1 clove of garlic, peeled
and crushed
12oz button mushrooms,
washed and sliced

Put the salt, pepper, mustard, oil, vinegar, parsley and garlic in a screw-topped jar. Shake well together. Pour over the prepared mushrooms in a bowl and leave to stand for an hour or more in the refrigerator. French dressing can be made in large quantities and kept covered in the refrigerator for 3 weeks.

Leek and red pepper salad

Metric	Imperial
Salt and freshly ground black pepper	Salt and freshly ground black pepper
Pinch dry English mustard	Pinch dry English mustard
3 × 15ml spoons olive or corn oil	3 tablespoons olive or corn oil
1 × 15ml spoon wine vinegar	1 tablespoon wine vinegar
450g leeks, washed, trimmed and sliced	1lb leeks, washed, trimmed and sliced
½ red pepper, washed, seeded and sliced into rings	½ red pepper, washed, seeded and sliced into rings

Make a French dressing by combining salt, pepper, mustard, oil and vinegar in a screw-topped jar. Shake well. Blanch leeks in boiling salted water for 5 minutes. Drain and allow to cool. Arrange leeks on a serving plate and top with rings of red pepper. Spoon French dressing over.

Cole slaw; Mushroom salad; Leek and red pepper salad

Tomato, onion and chive salad

Rice salad

Metric

225g long-grain rice,
washed
312g can mandarin
oranges, drained
3 spring onions, washed,
roots removed and finely
chopped
75g salted peanuts
Freshly ground black
pepper
5 × 15ml spoons
mayonnaise

Imperial

8oz long-grain rice,
washed
11oz can mandarin
oranges, drained
3 spring onions, washed,
roots removed and finely
chopped
3oz salted peanuts
Freshly ground black
pepper
5 tablespoons
mayonnaise

Cook rice in plenty of boiling salt water for about 10 minutes. Drain and run cold water through rice to separate grains. Transfer to a bowl. Stir in the mandarin oranges, spring onions and salted peanuts. Add plenty of freshly ground black pepper. Stir in the mayonnaise and serve chilled.

Apple and celery salad

Metric

Salt and freshly ground
black pepper
Pinch dry English mustard
3 × 15ml spoons olive or
corn oil
1 × 15ml spoon wine
vinegar
3 red eating apples, cored
and sliced
8 sticks celery, scrubbed
and chopped
50g walnuts, chopped

Imperial

Salt and freshly ground
black pepper
Pinch dry English mustard
3 tablespoons olive or
corn oil
1 tablespoon wine
vinegar
3 red eating apples, cored
and sliced
8 sticks celery, scrubbed
and chopped
2oz walnuts, chopped

This is a delicious winter salad. Put the salt, pepper, mustard, oil and vinegar in a screw-topped jar and shake well together. Put the apples and celery in a bowl with the chopped nuts. Pour over the French dressing and toss well so the apples and celery are well coated. Spoon into a serving dish and sprinkle with chopped parsley. A clove of garlic, peeled and crushed, may be included in the dressing.

To finish:
Chopped parsley, optional

To finish:
Chopped parsley, optional

Tomato, onion and chive salad

Metric	Imperial
Salt and freshly ground black pepper	Salt and freshly ground black pepper
Pinch dry English mustard	Pinch dry English mustard
2 × 15ml spoons olive or corn oil	2 tablespoons olive or corn oil
2 × 5ml spoons wine vinegar	2 teaspoons wine vinegar
2 medium-sized onions, peeled and sliced	2 medium-sized onions, peeled and sliced
Salt	Salt
6 firm tomatoes, peeled and thinly sliced	6 firm tomatoes, peeled and thinly sliced
2 × 5ml spoons chopped chives	2 teaspoons chopped chives

Make a French dressing as described in recipe for apple and celery salad, using salt, pepper, mustard, oil and vinegar. Lay onions on a tray and sprinkle liberally with salt and leave for 30 minutes. Drain and rinse under cold tap. Alternate tomato slices with onion rings on a plate. Add chopped chives to the French dressing and spoon over the vegetables.

Rice salad; Apple and celery salad

Tuna fish and tomato salad

Metric	Imperial
Salt and freshly ground black pepper	Salt and freshly ground black pepper
Pinch dry English mustard	Pinch dry English mustard
3 × 15ml spoons olive or corn oil	3 tablespoons olive or corn oil
1 × 15ml spoon wine vinegar	1 tablespoon wine vinegar
1 lettuce, washed and roughly cut into small pieces	1 lettuce, washed and roughly cut into small pieces
198g can tuna fish, drained and cut into chunks	7oz can tuna fish, drained and cut into chunks
2 tomatoes, peeled and quartered	2 tomatoes, peeled and quartered
50g frozen sweet corn, cooked and cooled	2oz frozen sweet corn, cooked and cooled
50g frozen French beans, cooked and cooled	2oz frozen French beans, cooked and cooled

Make a French dressing in a screw-topped jar by shaking together the salt, pepper, mustard, oil and vinegar. Place lettuce pieces in a salad bowl, add chunks of tuna fish, tomato wedges, corn and beans. Toss in the French dressing and serve.

Red kidney beans and onion

Metric	Imperial
Salt and freshly ground black pepper	Salt and freshly ground black pepper
Pinch dry English mustard	Pinch dry English mustard
½ teaspoon dried basil	½ teaspoon dried basil
1 clove of garlic, peeled and crushed	1 clove of garlic, peeled and crushed
3 × 15ml spoons olive or corn oil	3 tablespoons olive or corn oil
1 × 15ml spoon wine vinegar	1 tablespoon wine vinegar
1 small onion, peeled and thinly sliced	1 small onion, peeled and thinly sliced
Salt	Salt
432g can red kidney beans, drained	15¼oz can red kidney beans, drained

To finish:
Chopped parsley

To finish:
Chopped parsley

Make a French dressing by combining the salt, pepper, mustard, herbs, garlic, oil and vinegar in a screw-topped jar. Lay onion rings on a plate and sprinkle with salt. Leave for ½ an hour. Drain and rinse in cold water. Place beans in a bowl, sprinkle onion over the vegetables and toss in the herb French dressing. Garnish with plenty of chopped parsley.

Tuna fish and tomato salad; Red kidney beans and onion

Haddock with mustard sauce

Metric

¾kg haddock fillet,
skinned and cut into 4
Salt and freshly ground
black pepper
A little milk
20g butter
20g flour
300ml milk
2 × 15ml spoons French
mustard

To finish:
Chopped chives

Imperial

1½lb haddock fillet,
skinned and cut into 4
Salt and freshly ground
black pepper
A little milk
¾oz butter
¾oz flour
½ pint milk
2 tablespoons French
mustard

To finish:
Chopped chives

Cooking Time: 20 minutes
Oven: 160°C, 325°F, Gas Mark 3

Place the fish in an ovenproof serving dish. Pour a little milk over the fish and season. Cook covered in a slow oven for 15–20 minutes. Heat the butter, stir in the flour and cook for a couple of minutes. Allow to cool, then pour in the milk gradually. Bring to the boil stirring. Season and stir in the French mustard. Spoon the sauce over the fish and garnish with chopped chives. Serve with baked tomatoes and French beans.

Plaice in paprika and mushroom sauce

Metric

4 fillets of plaice, washed
300ml milk
Salt and freshly ground
black pepper
40g butter
50g button mushrooms,
washed and sliced
20g flour
2–3 × 5ml spoons paprika
pepper

To finish:
Watercress
Paprika pepper

Imperial

4 fillets of plaice, washed
½ pint milk
Salt and freshly ground
black pepper
1½oz butter
2oz button mushrooms,
washed and sliced
¾oz flour
2–3 teaspoons paprika
pepper

To finish:
Watercress
Paprika pepper

Cooking Time: 20 minutes
Oven 160°C, 325°F, Gas Mark 3

Put the plaice fillets in an ovenproof serving dish and pour a little milk over. Season lightly, cover and bake in a slow oven for 15–20 minutes. Heat butter, stir in mushrooms and cook until soft. Add the flour and paprika pepper and cook for a few minutes. Gradually add the remaining milk and any liquid left from the fish. Bring to the boil, stirring all the time. Season lightly. Pour over the fish and garnish with watercress and paprika pepper. Serve with buttered noodles and courgettes.

Stuffed cod cutlets

Metric

4 cod cutlets, washed,
trimmed of fins and
central bones removed
25g butter
½ onion, peeled and finely
chopped
4 rashers streaky bacon,
rinded and diced
2 tomatoes, skinned and
chopped
25g fresh white
breadcrumbs
2–3 × 15ml spoons milk
Salt and freshly ground
black pepper

To finish:
Grilled tomatoes
Parsley sprigs

Imperial

4 cod cutlets, washed,
trimmed of fins and
central bones removed
1oz butter
½ onion, peeled and finely
chopped
4 rashers streaky bacon,
rinded and diced
2 tomatoes, skinned and
chopped
1oz fresh white
breadcrumbs
2–3 tablespoons milk
Salt and freshly ground
black pepper

To finish:
Grilled tomatoes
Parsley sprigs

Cooking Time: 20 minutes
Oven: 160°C, 325°F, Gas Mark 3

Place fish in a buttered ovenproof dish. Heat the butter, fry the onion and bacon for a few minutes. Add the tomato and crumbs. Season well and fill the centre of each cutlet with the stuffing. Pour milk around the fish, cover and bake in a slow oven for about 20 minutes. Spoon cutlets onto a serving dish and serve garnished with grilled tomatoes and parsley sprigs.

Plaice in paprika and mushroom sauce; Haddock with mustard sauce; Stuffed cod cutlets; Cod and green pepper sauté

Cod and green pepper sauté

Metric

¾kg cod fillet, skinned
50g seasoned flour
2 rashers streaky bacon,
rinded and chopped
½ green pepper, seeded
and sliced
4 × 15ml spoons oil
3 tomatoes, skinned and
quartered
Salt and freshly ground
black pepper
50g Cheddar cheese,
grated

Imperial

1½lb cod fillet, skinned
2oz seasoned flour
2 rashers streaky bacon,
rinded and chopped
½ green pepper, seeded
and sliced
4 tablespoons oil
3 tomatoes, skinned and
quartered
Salt and freshly ground
black pepper
2oz Cheddar cheese,
grated

Cooking Time: 15–20 minutes

Cut the prepared fish into largish pieces and toss in seasoned flour. Lightly fry the bacon and pepper, add half the oil and half the fish. Turn occasionally to brown both sides, taking care not to break up. Remove from pan and drain. Heat the rest of the oil and fry remaining fish. Add prepared tomatoes and return all the ingredients to the pan to re-heat. Season with salt and freshly ground black pepper. Spoon into an ovenproof serving dish, top with grated cheese and brown under a hot grill. Serve immediately with creamed potatoes and buttered leeks.

Herrings with tomato sauce

Metric

4 medium-sized herrings,
washed, heads and tails
removed and cleaned
*Salt and freshly ground
black pepper*
25g butter, melted
For the sauce:
25g butter
*1 onion, peeled and finely
chopped*
*1 clove of garlic, peeled
and crushed*
396g can tomatoes
1 bay leaf
1 × 5ml spoon mixed herbs

To finish:
Lemon wedges
Cress

Imperial

4 medium-sized herrings,
washed, heads and tails
removed and cleaned
*Salt and freshly ground
black pepper*
1oz butter, melted
For the sauce:
1oz butter
*1 onion, peeled and finely
chopped*
*1 clove of garlic, peeled
and crushed*
14oz can tomatoes
1 bay leaf
1 teaspoon mixed herbs

To finish:
Lemon wedges
Cress

Cooking Time: 10–15 minutes

Line grill pan with aluminium foil. Make 2–3 diagonal cuts in the flesh on both sides of the fish and season. Brush with melted butter and grill on the foil for 10 minutes, turning once. For the tomato sauce, heat the butter and fry the onion with the garlic until soft. Add tomatoes, bay leaf, herbs and season well. Bring to the boil and simmer until thickened. Remove bay leaf and serve in a sauce boat. Transfer fish to a serving dish, garnish with lemon wedges and cress. Serve with grilled mushrooms.

Saturday fish pie

Metric

¾ kg fresh cod or haddock
or coley, skinned
*Salt and freshly ground
black pepper*
1 bay leaf
¾ kg old potatoes, peeled
15 g butter
A little milk
25 g butter
25 g flour
150 ml milk
*1 × 15 ml spoon chopped
parsley*
*2 hard-boiled eggs,
chopped*
*Finely grated rind of
1 lemon*
*1 × 15 ml spoon lemon
juice*
*¼ teaspoon cayenne
pepper*
*1 × 15 ml spoon chopped
chives*
*25 g Cheddar cheese,
grated*

Imperial

1½ lb fresh cod or haddock
or coley, skinned
*Salt and freshly ground
black pepper*
1 bay leaf
1½ lb old potatoes, peeled
½ oz butter
A little milk
1 oz butter
1 oz flour
¼ pint milk
*1 tablespoon chopped
parsley*
*2 hard-boiled eggs,
chopped*
*Finely grated rind of
1 lemon*
*1 tablespoon lemon
juice*
*¼ teaspoon cayenne
pepper*
*1 tablespoon chopped
chives*
*1 oz Cheddar cheese,
grated*

Cooking time: 30 minutes
Oven: 190°C, 375°F, Gas Mark 5

Poach fish in water seasoned with salt, black pepper and bayleaf for 10–15 minutes. Drain, retaining 150 ml/¼ pint of cooking liquid. Cook potatoes, mash and add butter and milk and seasoning. Allow to cool. Make a white sauce using butter and flour, milk and cooking liquid from fish (see recipe for Cauliflower au gratin, page 20). Flake fish and add to sauce with parsley, chopped egg, lemon rind and juice, cayenne pepper and chives. Season. Spoon into a 900 ml/1½ pint pie dish. Sprinkle grated cheese over the top. Pipe creamed potato over fish mixture using a 1cm ½ inch star vegetable nozzle. Bake in a moderately hot oven for 20–30 minutes. Serve with peas and baked tomatoes.

Mackerel with lemon and orange stuffing

Metric

2 oranges, peeled and
roughly chopped
½ onion, peeled and finely
chopped
50g fresh white
breadcrumbs
1 × 15ml spoon chopped
parsley
Finely grated rind of 1
lemon
2 × 15ml spoons lemon
juice
Salt and freshly ground
black pepper
4 medium-sized mackerel,
washed, cleaned and fins
trimmed

To finish:
Lemon slices

Imperial

2 oranges, peeled and
roughly chopped
½ onion, peeled and finely
chopped
2oz fresh white
breadcrumbs
1 tablespoon chopped
parsley
Finely grated rind of 1
lemon
2 tablespoons lemon
juice
Salt and freshly ground
black pepper
4 medium-sized mackerel,
washed, cleaned and fins
trimmed

To finish:
Lemon slices

Cooking Time: 30–35 minutes
Oven: 170°C, 325°F, Gas Mark 3

Line an ovenproof dish with buttered foil. Mix the orange, onions, breadcrumbs, parsley, lemon rind and juice together. Season well. Fill the fish with the stuffing and place on the foil. Cover loosely with foil and bake in a slow oven for 30–35 minutes. Place mackerel on a serving dish, garnish with lemon slices and serve with a tossed green salad.

Herrings with tomato sauce; Saturday fish pie; Mackerel with lemon and orange stuffing

Meat can either be roasted in the oven or on a spit. If the oven method is chosen a fast or slow oven can be used. A fast or hot oven, 200°C, 400°F, Gas Mark 6, will seal the outer surface of the meat quickly, which retains all the succulent meat juices. The slow oven, 180°C, 350°F, Gas Mark 4, tends to produce a more tender joint with less shrinkage, but the flavour is not quite as good. It is important to baste the meat well while cooking, spooning over the hot fat and juices from the tin.

Only prime cuts of meat should be roasted. Find a butcher who sells good quality meat which has been properly hung so it will have a good flavour. Choose joints which have a fresh appearance and are not too fatty. Ask the butcher's advice if you are in doubt, as he can suggest the best cut for a particular cooking method.

Stuffed roast turkey

This guide will give you a good idea of what size bird to buy for your requirements.

3–4kg (6–8lb), oven ready turkey gives 8–10 servings
4–6kg (8–12lb), oven ready turkey gives 10–15 servings
$6\frac{1}{2}$–$7\frac{1}{2}$kg (14–16lb), oven ready turkey gives 18–22
   servings

If the turkey is a fresh one cover loosely with foil and leave in the refrigerator until required. If the bird is frozen, remove from its wrappings and cover loosely with foil or muslin, and thaw in a cool place for $1\frac{1}{2}$–3 days, depending on its size.

A turkey can be roasted in a slow or fast oven. Cooking times for the slow method at 160°C, 325°F, Gas Mark 3 are:

3–4kg (6–8lb) takes $3\frac{1}{2}$ hours
4–6kg (8–12lb) takes $3\frac{1}{2}$–4 hours
6–$7\frac{1}{2}$kg (12–16lb) takes 4–$4\frac{1}{2}$ hours

Cooking times for the fast method, using foil at 230°C, 450°F, Gas Mark 8 are:

3–4kg (6–8lb) takes $2\frac{1}{2}$ hours
4–6kg (8–12lb) takes $2\frac{1}{2}$–$2\frac{3}{4}$ hours
6–$7\frac{1}{2}$kg (12–16lb) takes $2\frac{3}{4}$–$3\frac{1}{4}$ hours

Roasting meat

Roasting Times and Temperatures
200°C, 400°F, Gas Mark 6

Beef	15–20 minutes per $\frac{1}{2}$kg (1lb) +	15–20 minutes over
Lamb	20 minutes per $\frac{1}{2}$kg (1lb) +	20 minutes over
Pork	25 minutes per $\frac{1}{2}$kg (1lb) +	25 minutes over
Veal	20 minutes per $\frac{1}{2}$kg (1lb) +	20 minutes over
Chicken	20 minutes per $\frac{1}{2}$kg (1lb) +	15 minutes over

Spit Roasting Times are roughly the same as above
180°C, 350°F, Gas Mark 4

Beef	27 minutes per $\frac{1}{2}$kg (1lb) +	27 minutes over
Lamb	27 minutes per $\frac{1}{2}$kg (1lb) +	27 minutes over
Pork	35 minutes per $\frac{1}{2}$kg (1lb) +	35 minutes over
Veal	Fast roasting only recommended.	
Chicken	Fast roasting only recommended.	

Chicken can be French roasted by beating some mixed herbs into a knob of butter and placing inside the bird. Place in a roasting tin, pour over 300ml ($\frac{1}{2}$ pint) stock and cook at 180°C, 375°F, Gas Mark 5 for 25 minutes to $\frac{1}{2}$kg (1lb).

Sage and onion

Metric	Imperial	Cooking Time: 5 minutes
50g butter 2 onions, peeled and finely chopped 2 × 5ml spoons dried sage 100g fresh white breadcrumbs Salt and freshly ground black pepper	2oz butter 2 onions, peeled and finely chopped 2 teaspoons dried sage 4oz fresh white breadcrumbs Salt and freshly ground black pepper	Heat butter and fry onions until soft. Add the sage, breadcrumbs and seasoning. Use with pork.

Chestnut and sausage

Metric	Imperial	Cooking Time: 5 minutes
25g butter ½ onion, peeled and finely chopped 250g chestnut purée 150g pork sausage meat 100g fresh white breadcrumbs 1 × 15ml spoon finely chopped parsley Salt and freshly ground black pepper	1oz butter ½ onion, peeled and finely chopped 8oz chestnut purée 6oz pork sausage meat 4oz fresh white breadcrumbs 1 tablespoon finely chopped parsley Salt and freshly ground black pepper	Heat butter and fry onion until soft. Pour into the chestnut purée and add sausage meat. Stir in breadcrumbs and parsley. Season lightly. Use to stuff turkey.

Thyme and parsley

Metric	Imperial	
75g margarine 150g fresh white breadcrumbs 2 × 5ml spoons chopped fresh thyme 2 × 15ml spoons chopped fresh parsley Finely grated rind of ½ lemon Salt and freshly ground black pepper	3oz margarine 6oz fresh white breadcrumbs 2 teaspoons chopped fresh thyme 2 tablespoons chopped fresh parsley Finely grated rind of ½ lemon Salt and freshly ground black pepper	Rub margarine into breadcrumbs. Add thyme, parsley, lemon rind and seasoning. Bind together and use to stuff poultry.

Mushroom

Metric	Imperial	Cooking Time: 5 minutes
25g margarine 1 medium-sized onion, peeled and finely chopped 100g mushrooms, washed and chopped 1 × 15ml spoon finely chopped parsley 100g fresh white breadcrumbs Finely grated rind of ½ lemon Salt and freshly ground black pepper 1 egg, beaten	1oz margarine 1 medium-sized onion, peeled and finely chopped 4oz mushrooms, washed and chopped 1 tablespoon finely chopped parsley 4oz fresh white breadcrumbs Finely grated rind of ½ lemon Salt and freshly ground black pepper 1 egg, beaten	Heat margarine and fry onion and mushrooms until soft. Add parsley, breadcrumbs, lemon rind and seasoning. Bind with a little beaten egg. Use to stuff poultry.

Thyme and parsley; Mushroom; Chestnut and sausage; Sage and onion

Pork and beef loaf

Metric

225g minced beef
350g minced pork
4 × 15ml spoons thyme
and parsley stuffing mix
1 × 15ml spoon
Worcestershire sauce
1 × 15ml spoon tomato
ketchup
1 onion, peeled and finely
chopped
1 clove garlic, peeled and
crushed
Salt and freshly ground
black pepper
1 egg, beaten

Tomato Sauce:
2 × 5ml spoons cornflour
396g can tomatoes
Salt and freshly ground
black pepper

Imperial

8oz minced beef
12oz minced pork
4 tablespoons thyme and
parsley stuffing mix
1 tablespoon
Worcestershire sauce
1 tablespoon tomato
ketchup
1 onion, peeled and finely
chopped
1 clove garlic, peeled and
crushed
Salt and freshly ground
black pepper
1 egg, beaten

Tomato Sauce:
2 teaspoons cornflour
14oz can tomatoes
Salt and freshly ground
black pepper

Cooking Time: 1 hour
Oven: 180°C, 350°F, Gas Mark 4

Place all ingredients, but for the egg, in a large bowl and combine well together. Stir the beaten egg into the mixture and spoon the contents into a greased 1kg (2lb) loaf tin. Cover with foil and bake in the centre of a moderate oven for 1 hour. Serve hot with tomato sauce, or cold with salad and French bread.

Tomato Sauce: Blend the cornflour with a little juice from the canned tomatoes, in a saucepan. Add the rest of the juice and tomatoes and bring to the boil stirring until clear. Taste and adjust the seasoning.

Paprika beef

Metric

40g margarine
¾kg stewing steak,
trimmed of excess fat
and cubed
1 onion, peeled and sliced
1 clove of garlic, peeled
and crushed
1 × 15ml spoon paprika
 pepper
2 × 5ml spoons tomato
purée
25g flour
450ml beef stock
Salt and freshly ground
black pepper
Bouquet garni
½ green pepper, seeded
and sliced
2 tomatoes, skinned and
quartered

To finish:
142g carton soured cream
Chopped parsley

Imperial

1½oz margarine
1¼lb stewing steak,
trimmed of excess fat
and cubed
1 onion, peeled and sliced
1 clove of garlic, peeled
and crushed
1 tablespoon paprika
pepper
2 teaspoons tomato
purée
1oz flour
¾ pint beef stock
Salt and freshly ground
black pepper
Bouquet garni
½ green pepper, seeded
and sliced
2 tomatoes, skinned and
quartered

To finish:
5oz carton soured cream
Chopped parsley

Cooking Time: 2½ hours
Oven: 150°C, 300°F, Gas Mark 2

Heat 25g (1oz) of the margarine and fry the meat lightly on all sides. Remove, drain on kitchen paper and place in casserole dish. Heat the rest of the margarine, fry the onion and garlic lightly, then stir in the paprika pepper, tomato purée and flour. Cook for a minute, then slowly add the beef stock. Bring to the boil stirring all the time, season well, add bouquet garni and pour over the meat in the casserole dish. Cover and cook in a slow oven for about 2 hours. Add the pepper and tomatoes and cook a further 30 minutes. Just before serving stir in the soured cream. Taste and adjust seasoning. Garnish with a little chopped parsley and serve with a green salad and buttered potatoes.

Pork and beef loaf; Beef casserole; Paprika beef

Beef casserole

Metric

3 × 15ml spoons oil
¾kg stewing steak,
trimmed of excess fat
and cut into 2.5cm cubes
2 leeks, trimmed, washed
and thickly sliced
2 carrots, peeled and
sliced
1 large onion, peeled and
sliced
25g flour
450ml beef stock
396g can tomatoes
Salt and freshly ground
black pepper

Imperial

3 tablespoons oil
1½lb stewing steak,
trimmed of excess fat
and cut into 1in cubes
2 leeks, trimmed, washed
and thickly sliced
2 carrots, peeled and
sliced
1 large onion, peeled and
sliced
1oz flour
¾ pint beef stock
14oz can tomatoes
Salt and freshly ground
black pepper

Cooking Time: 2½ hours
Oven: 150°C, 300°F, Gas Mark 2

Heat the oil in a saucepan and fry the meat briskly on all sides. Remove, drain and place in a casserole dish. Add the leeks and carrots to the meat. Re-heat the remaining oil in the pan and fry the onion until soft. Sprinkle the flour into the pan and cook for 1 minute. Allow to cool slightly then pour in the stock gradually. Bring to the boil stirring constantly. Add the tomatoes and season well. Pour the tomato onion sauce into the casserole dish, cover and cook in a slow oven for about 2½ hours. Serve with baked potatoes and French beans.

Steak, kidney and soya pie

Metric

100g T.V.P. Beef Chunks
300ml beef stock
225g stewing steak,
trimmed of excess fat
and cut into 2.5cm cubes
4 lamb's or ox kidneys,
trimmed, cleaned and
cubed
25g seasoned flour
1 medium-sized onion,
peeled and sliced
50g mushrooms, washed
and sliced
1 × 15ml spoon finely
chopped parsley
Salt and freshly ground
black pepper
198g bought puff pastry
1 egg, beaten

Imperial

4oz T.V.P. Beef Chunks
½ pint beef stock
8oz stewing steak,
trimmed of excess fat
and cut into 1in cubes
4 lamb's or ox kidneys,
trimmed, cleaned and
cubed
1oz seasoned flour
1 medium-sized onion,
peeled and sliced
2oz mushrooms, washed
and sliced
1 tablespoon finely
chopped parsley
Salt and freshly ground
black pepper
7oz bought puff pastry
1 egg, beaten

Cooking Time: 2 hours
Oven: 220°C, 425°F, Gas Mark 7

Soya bean protein is an economical extender to fresh meat. Use it in Bolognese sauces and curries too. Reconstitute the T.V.P. Beef Chunks in the beef stock. Toss the pieces of stewing steak and kidney in seasoned flour and place in a 900ml (1½ pint) pie dish. Drain the reconstituted T.V.P. Beef Chunks retaining the liquid and add to the steak and kidney in the dish. Sprinkle onion, mushrooms and parsley over the meat, season well. Pour over the remaining stock. Roll out the pastry and top the pie. Trim and flute the edges. Use pastry trimmings to make leaves for decorating the pie. Glaze with beaten egg and cook in a hot oven for 25 minutes. Cover pastry with foil and reduce heat to 180°C, 350°F, Gas Mark 4 for a further 1½ hours. Serve hot with braised leeks.

Burgundy pot roast

Metric

1¼–1½kg topside or
aitchbone of beef
Salt and freshly ground
black pepper
25g butter
1 onion, peeled and sliced
2 carrots, peeled and
sliced
2 sticks celery, scrubbed
and chopped
1 clove of garlic, peeled
and crushed
150ml Burgundy
150ml beef stock
Bouquet garni
1 bay leaf

To finish:
Watercress sprigs

Imperial

2½–3lb topside or
aitchbone of beef
Salt and freshly ground
black pepper
1oz butter
1 onion, peeled and sliced
2 carrots, peeled and
sliced
2 sticks celery, scrubbed
and chopped
1 clove of garlic, peeled
and crushed
¼ pint Burgundy
¼ pint beef stock
Bouquet garni
1 bay leaf

To finish:
Watercress sprigs

Cooking Time: 2–2½ hours
Oven: 160°C, 325°F, Gas Mark 3

This is an excellent way to cook the less tender cuts of beef and retains all the flavour and juices of the meat. Season the joint well with salt and freshly ground black pepper. Heat butter in a flameproof casserole and quickly fry the meat all over to brown it lightly. Remove and place on one side. Add the onion, carrots, celery and garlic to the pan and cook for a couple of minutes. Replace the meat on top of the vegetables, pour the wine and stock over. Add the bouquet garni and bay leaf and season lightly. Cover and cook in a slow oven for about 2–2½ hours. Place joint on a serving plate. Spoon the vegetables around the meat. Remove bouquet garni and bay leaf. Reduce the liquid in the pan until slightly thickened, pour over the meat or serve separately. Garnish with watercress sprigs and serve with braised leeks.

Lamb chops in wine sauce

Metric	Imperial	Cooking Time: 45 minutes

Metric	Imperial
25g margarine	1oz margarine
4 loin of lamb chops	4 loin of lamb chops
1 onion, peeled and sliced	1 onion, peeled and sliced
1–2 × 5 ml spoons paprika	1–2 teaspoons paprika
150ml dry white wine	¼ pint dry white wine
150ml chicken stock	¼ pint chicken stock
1 × 15ml spoon medium sherry	1 tablespoon medium sherry
Salt and freshly ground black pepper	Salt and freshly ground black pepper
1 × 5ml spoon cornflour	1 teaspoon cornflour
50g button mushrooms, washed and sliced	2 oz button mushrooms, washed and sliced
2 tomatoes, skinned	2 tomatoes, skinned
4 × 15ml spoons single cream (optional)	4 tablespoons single cream (optional)

Heat margarine and brown chops on each side. Drain and leave on one side. Add onion to pan and cook until soft, with the paprika pepper. Allow to cool slightly then pour on wine, stock and sherry. Return chops to pan, season well, bring to the boil, reduce heat and simmer chops, covered, for about 30 minutes. Blend cornflour with a little cold water and stir into wine and stock, stirring all the time. Add prepared mushrooms and quartered tomatoes. Taste and adjust seasoning and simmer for a further 15 minutes, stir in cream if used. Place chops on a serving dish and spoon over sauce. Garnish with chopped parsley if liked, and serve with buttered French beans.

Apricot stuffed shoulder of lamb

Cooking Time: 2 hours
Oven: 180°C, 350°F, Gas Mark 4

Metric	Imperial
75g dried apricots,	3oz dried apricots,
75g fresh breadcrumbs	3oz fresh breadcrumbs
1 × 15ml spoon finely chopped parsley	1 tablespoon finely chopped parsley
½ teaspoon dried thyme	½ teaspoon dried thyme
Salt and freshly ground black pepper	Salt and freshly ground black pepper
1 × 15ml spoon lemon juice	1 tablespoon lemon juice
25g butter	1oz butter
1 small egg, beaten	1 small egg, beaten
1½kg shoulder of lamb, boned	3–3½lb shoulder of lamb, boned
1 × 15ml spoon flour	1 tablespoon flour
300ml vegetable water or stock	½ pint vegetable water or stock

To finish:
Watercress

To finish:
Watercress

Bring dried apricots to the boil in a little water, and allow to simmer for 5 minutes. Drain, allow to cool and chop finely. Add to breadcrumbs with parsley, thyme, salt, freshly ground black pepper and lemon juice. Heat butter over a low heat and pour into stuffing ingredients. Combine well and bind together with the beaten egg. Season lamb well and spread prepared stuffing over surface. Roll up tightly and secure with string at intervals. Bake in a moderate oven for about 2 hours, until lightly browned. Place on a hot serving dish. Pour off excess fat from roasting tin, stir in flour and cook for a couple of minutes. Allow to cool before adding water from vegetables or stock, gradually, and bring to the boil stirring all the time. Taste and adjust seasoning and serve gravy in a sauce boat. Remove string from joint and serve garnished with watercress.

Country lamb casserole

Cooking Time: 2 hours
Oven: 170°C, 325°F, Gas Mark 3

Metric	Imperial
1kg best end of neck of lamb	2lb best end of neck of lamb
225g onions, peeled and sliced	8oz onions, peeled and sliced
450g carrots, scraped and chopped	1lb carrots, scraped and chopped
¾kg potatoes, peeled and thickly sliced	1½lb potatoes, peeled and thickly sliced
Salt and freshly ground black pepper	Salt and freshly ground black pepper
½ teaspoon dried thyme	½ teaspoon dried thyme
900ml boiling water	1½ pints boiling water

To finish:
Chopped parsley

To finish:
Chopped parsley

Cut neck into chops and season well. Put alternative layers of vegetables and meat in a large casserole dish and finish with a layer of potato. Season well between the layers and sprinkle the herbs at the same time. Pour the water over the meat, cover and cook in a slow oven for about 2 hours. Just before serving, skim and sprinkle well with parsley. Serve with buttered cabbage.

Lamb chops in wine sauce; Apricot stuffed shoulder of lamb; Country lamb casserole

Pork fillet with apricots

Metric

450g pork fillet, cut into bite-size pieces
2 × 15ml spoons seasoned flour
50g butter
396g can apricot halves, drained and juice retained
2 × 15ml spoons Worcestershire sauce
2 × 15ml spoons Demerara sugar
2 × 5ml spoons vinegar
2 × 5ml spoons lemon juice
8 × 15ml spoons water
225g long grain rice

Imperial

1lb pork fillet, cut into bite-size pieces
2 tablespoons seasoned flour
2oz butter
14oz can apricot halves, drained and juice retained
2 tablespoons Worcestershire sauce
2 tablespoons Demerara sugar
2 teaspoons vinegar
2 teaspoons lemon juice
8 tablespoons water
8oz long grain rice

Cooking Time: 20 minutes

Toss pork pieces in seasoned flour. Heat butter and fry pork until lightly browned. Chop all but 3 apricot halves. Mix 8 × 15ml spoons (8 tablespoons) apricot juice with Worcestershire sauce, sugar, vinegar, lemon juice and water. Add any remaining flour to the pork and pour in the apricot sauce and chopped fruit. Bring to the boil stirring. Reduce heat, cover and simmer for about 15 minutes. Spoon pork and sauce onto a serving dish. Cook the rice in boiling, salted water and border around the meat. Garnish with remaining apricot halves.

Pork fillet with apricots

Pork chops in orange sauce

Metric

4 pork chops, trimmed of
excess fat
Salt and freshly ground
black pepper
2 × 5ml spoons dried sage
25g butter
1 clove of garlic, peeled
and crushed
15g cornflour
300ml chicken stock
6 × 15ml spoons orange
juice
2 fresh oranges, peeled,
pith removed and
segmented

To finish:
Watercress

Imperial

4 pork chops, trimmed of
excess fat
Salt and freshly ground
black pepper
2 teaspoons dried sage
1oz butter
1 clove of garlic, peeled
and crushed
½oz cornflour
½ pint chicken stock
6 tablespoons orange juice
2 fresh oranges, peeled,
pith removed and
segmented

To finish:
Watercress

Cooking Time: 45 minutes

Season chops with salt and pepper and sprinkle sage over
each one. Heat butter in a pan and fry garlic for a minute,
then brown the chops on both sides. Remove and leave on
one side. Stir the cornflour into the remaining fat in the pan
and cook for a few minutes. Gradually add the stock and
orange juice and bring to the boil. Return the chops to the
pan, reduce heat, add the segments from one orange, cover
and cook for about 40 minutes. Taste sauce and adjust
seasoning. Place chops on a serving plate with orange
pieces, pour sauce over and serve garnished with segments
from the remaining orange, and watercress.

Pork chops in orange sauce

Stuffed liver braise

Metric	Imperial
450g lamb's liver	1lb lamb's liver
1 onion, peeled and chopped	1 onion, peeled and chopped
1 × 15ml spoon finely chopped parsley	1 tablespoon finely chopped parsley
150g fresh white breadcrumbs	5oz fresh white breadcrumbs
Salt and freshly ground black pepper	Salt and freshly ground black pepper
Finely grated rind of 1 lemon	Finely grated rind of 1 lemon
3 × 5ml spoons tomato ketchup	3 teaspoons tomato ketchup
Beaten egg to bind	Beaten egg to bind
8 rashers streaky bacon	8 rashers streaky bacon
125ml beef stock	¼ pint beef stock
1 × 5ml spoon cornflour	1 teaspoon cornflour

Cooking Time: 40 minutes
Oven: 180°C, 350°F, Gas Mark 4

Lay eight slices of washed, trimmed liver in an ovenproof dish. In a bowl combine onion, parsley, breadcrumbs, seasoning, lemon rind and tomato ketchup. Add a little beaten egg and bind together. Spread a little stuffing to cover each slice of liver. Top each with a rasher of bacon with rind removed. Pour stock around liver, cover dish with foil and cook in a moderate oven for about 40 minutes. Blend the cornflour with a little cold water in a pan. Strain the stock from the liver and pour into the blended cornflour. Bring to the boil, stirring all the time, taste and adjust seasoning and pour over liver. Serve hot with buttered corn kernels and jacket potatoes.

Sausage and kidney casserole

Metric	Imperial
450g chipolata sausages	1lb chipolata sausages
4 lamb's kidneys, skinned, trimmed and halved	4 lamb's kidneys, skinned, trimmed and halved
1 onion, peeled and sliced	1 onion, peeled and sliced
25g flour	1oz flour
300ml dry cider	½ pint dry cider
300ml beef stock	½ pint beef stock
Salt and freshly ground black pepper	Salt and freshly ground black pepper
2 sticks celery, scrubbed and chopped	2 sticks celery, scrubbed and chopped
2 carrots, peeled and sliced	2 carrots, peeled and sliced
Bouquet garni	Bouquet garni

Cooking Time: 1 hour
Oven: 180°C, 350°F, Gas Mark 4

This is an economical, nutritious dish, and delicious too. Fry sausages until lightly browned. Remove from the pan and place in a casserole dish. Lightly fry the kidneys, then transfer to casserole. Fry the onion for a couple of minutes in the remaining fat in the pan. Add the flour, cook for 2 minutes, then gradually pour on the cider and stock. Bring to the boil, stirring. Season well. Put the rest of the vegetables into the casserole and pour over the cider sauce. Add a bouquet garni, cover and cook for about 1 hour. Remove bouquet garni. Serve with boiled potatoes and buttered leeks.

Liver stroganoff

Metric	Imperial
450g lamb's liver	1lb lamb's liver
40g seasoned flour	1½oz seasoned flour
75g margarine	3oz margarine
1 onion, peeled and finely chopped	1 onion, peeled and finely chopped
2 rashers streaky bacon, rinded and chopped	2 rashers streaky bacon, rinded and chopped
100g button mushrooms, washed and sliced	4oz button mushrooms, washed and sliced
150ml chicken stock	¼ pint chicken stock
Salt and freshly ground black pepper	Salt and freshly ground black pepper
142g carton soured cream	5oz carton soured cream

Cooking Time: 15–20 minutes

Cut the trimmed liver into 5cm (2in) strips. Toss the liver in seasoned flour. Heat half the margarine in a frying pan and fry liver until lightly browned – about 5 minutes. Remove from pan and put on one side. Add remaining margarine to pan and fry onion, bacon and mushrooms until soft. Stir in remainder of seasoned flour and cook for 2 minutes. Allow to cool slightly, then pour in stock gradually and bring to the boil, stirring. Season well, return liver to the pan and cook for a further 5 minutes. Off the heat stir in the soured cream and re-heat without boiling. Garnish with chopped chives and serve with boiled rice, French beans and grilled tomatoes.

To finish:	To finish:
Chopped chives	Chopped chives

Stuffed liver braise; Sausage and kidney casserole; Liver stroganoff

Asparagus chicken pie

Metric

50g packet asparagus soup
450ml water
350g cooked chicken,
sliced
50g button mushrooms,
washed and sliced
Salt and freshly ground
black pepper
225g bought puff pastry
Beaten egg to glaze

Imperial

2oz packet asparagus soup
¾ pint water
12oz cooked chicken,
sliced
2oz button mushrooms,
washed and sliced
Salt and freshly ground
black pepper
8oz bought puff pastry
Beaten egg to glaze

Cooking Time: 30 minutes
Oven: 220°C, 425°F, Gas Mark 7

Empty contents of packet of soup into a saucepan. Add cold water and slowly bring to the boil, stirring. Stir in chicken and mushrooms, season and pour into a 1¼l (2 pint) pie dish. Allow to cool. Roll out pastry and top the pie. Make leaves with pastry trimmings and decorate pastry top. Brush with beaten egg and cook in a hot oven for about 25–30 minutes. Cover with foil if pastry is browning too quickly. Serve hot with French beans and boiled potatoes.

Pot roasted chicken with vegetables

Metric

50g butter
1 large onion, peeled and
sliced
3 carrots, peeled and cut
into wedges
3 sticks celery, scrubbed
and chopped
3 rashers streaky bacon,
rinded and chopped
½ teaspoon dried thyme
1 × 1¾kg oven-ready
chicken
Salt and freshly ground
black pepper

To finish:
Watercress

Imperial

2oz butter
1 large onion, peeled and
sliced
3 carrots, peeled and cut
into wedges
3 sticks celery, scrubbed
and chopped
3 rashers streaky bacon,
rinded and chopped
½ teaspoon dried thyme
1 × 3½lb oven-ready
chicken
Salt and freshly ground
black pepper

To finish:
Watercress

Cooking Time: 2 hours
Oven: 150°C, 300°F, Gas Mark 2

Melt 25g (1oz) butter in a large flameproof casserole or pan. Add onion, carrots, celery, and bacon and fry for 5 minutes, stirring occasionally. Remove and drain on kitchen paper. Heat the rest of the butter and brown the chicken all over. Remove pan from the heat and spoon the vegetables around the bird. Season lightly, sprinkle with the thyme, cover and cook in a slow oven for about 2 hours.
To finish: Place the chicken on a serving dish, spoon the vegetables around. Skim off the fat from juices, bring to the boil and pour over the chicken or serve separately in a sauce boat. Garnish with watercress.

Chicken in pepper and mushroom sauce

Metric

50g butter
100g button mushrooms,
washed and sliced
½ green pepper, seeded
and sliced
2 × 15ml spoons flour
300ml chicken stock
150ml milk
Salt and freshly ground
black pepper
350g cooked chicken,
sliced

Imperial

2oz butter
4oz button mushrooms,
washed and sliced
½ green pepper, seeded
and sliced
2 tablespoons flour
½ pint chicken stock
¼ pint milk
Salt and freshly ground
black pepper
12oz cooked chicken,
sliced

Cooking Time: 30 minutes
Oven: 180°C, 350°F, Gas Mark 4

Heat the butter in a pan and fry the mushrooms and pepper for a few minutes. Stir in the flour and cook slowly for 2 minutes. Allow to cool slightly, then gradually pour in the stock and milk stirring all the time. Bring to the boil and season well. Off the heat stir in the chicken and transfer to a casserole, cover and cook in a moderate oven for about 30 minutes. Serve hot with baked potatoes and buttered courgettes.

Chicken in pepper and mushroom sauce; Asparagus chicken pie; Pot roasted chicken with vegetables

Quick cassoulet

Metric	Imperial
2 × 15ml spoons oil	2 tablespoons oil
4 chicken or duck portions	4 chicken or duck portions
2 onions, peeled and sliced	2 onions, peeled and sliced
2 rashers streaky bacon, rinded and chopped	2 rashers streaky bacon, rinded and chopped
1 clove of garlic, peeled and crushed	1 clove of garlic, peeled and crushed
150ml dry white wine	¼ pint dry white wine
300ml chicken stock	½ pint chicken stock
1 × 15ml spoon tomato ketchup	1 tablespoon tomato ketchup
175g garlic sausage, diced	6oz garlic sausage, diced
1 × 5ml spoon dried thyme	1 teaspoon dried thyme
1 bay leaf	1 bay leaf
439g can baked beans in tomato sauce	15½oz can baked beans in tomato sauce
Salt and freshly ground black pepper	Salt and freshly ground black pepper
2 × 15ml spoons cornflour	2 tablespoons cornflour
3 × 15ml spoons water	3 tablespoons water

To finish:

Metric	Imperial
4 × 15ml spoons finely chopped parsley	4 tablespoons finely chopped parsley
100g fresh white breadcrumbs	4oz fresh white breadcrumbs

Cooking Time: 1 hour 20 minutes
Oven: 180°C, 350°F, Gas Mark 4 then: 220°C, 425°F, Gas Mark 7

Heat the oil and fry the chicken (or duck), portions until lightly browned. Drain and place in a casserole dish. Fry the onions, bacon and garlic for a few minutes and spoon over the chicken pieces. Combine the wine and stock and stir in the tomato ketchup. Pour over the chicken portions and add the garlic sausage, thyme, bay leaf and the contents of the can of baked beans. Season well. Cover and cook in a moderate oven for an hour. Blend the cornflour with the cold water and stir into the cassoulet.

To finish: Mix the parsley and breadcrumbs together and sprinkle over the surface of the dish. Return to the oven and cook in a hot oven for 20 minutes until topping is crisp and lightly browned. Serve hot with boiled potatoes and a green salad.

Chicken in sweet and sour sauce

Metric	Imperial
8 chicken drumsticks	8 chicken drumsticks
Salt and freshly ground black pepper	Salt and freshly ground black pepper
2 × 5ml spoons powdered ginger	2 teaspoons powdered ginger
25g butter for grilling	1oz butter for grilling
2 × 15ml spoons cornflour	2 tablespoons cornflour
Cold water	Cold water
5 × 15ml spoons vinegar	5 tablespoons vinegar
2 × 5ml spoons soy sauce	2 teaspoons soy sauce
3–4 × 15ml spoons brown sugar	3–4 tablespoons brown sugar
300ml chicken stock	½ pint chicken stock
398g can pineapple pieces	11oz can pineapple pieces
4 tomatoes, skinned and quartered	4 tomatoes, skinned and quartered
1 red pepper, seeded and sliced	1 red pepper, seeded and sliced

To finish:

Metric	Imperial
Boiled rice	Boiled rice

Cooking Time: 30 minutes
Oven: 180°C, 350°F, Gas Mark 4

Season chicken with salt and freshly ground black pepper. Rub ginger into surface of each joint and dot each with a knob of butter. Grill until golden and transfer to a casserole dish. In a pan blend cornflour with a little cold water, stir in vinegar, soy sauce, sugar and chicken stock. Bring slowly to the boil, stirring until sauce thickens. Stir in the contents of the can of pineapple, the tomatoes and red pepper. Pour sauce over chicken joints, cover and cook for about 30 minutes. Serve in a border of boiled rice.

Chicken in sweet and sour sauce; Quick cassoulet; Rabbit pie

Rabbit pie

Metric

40g margarine
4 rabbit joints
1 onion, peeled and sliced
2 carrots, peeled and sliced
2 rashers streaky bacon, rinded and chopped
1 × 15ml spoon flour
150ml dry white wine
300ml chicken stock
1 × 5ml spoon French mustard
Bouquet garni
Salt and freshly ground black pepper
1 × 15ml spoon chopped parsley
175g bought puff pastry
Beaten egg for glazing

Imperial

1½oz margarine
4 rabbit joints
1 onion, peeled and sliced
2 carrots, peeled and sliced
2 rashers streaky bacon, rinded and chopped
1 tablespoon flour
¼ pint dry white wine
½ pint chicken stock
1 teaspoon French mustard
Bouquet garni
Salt and freshly ground black pepper
1 tablespoon chopped parsley
6oz bought puff pastry
Beaten egg for glazing

Cooking Time: 1½ hours
Oven: 220°C, 425°F, Gas Mark 7
Reduce to: 180°C, 350°F, Gas Mark 4

Rabbit provides a delicate alternative to chicken. Heat margarine and fry rabbit joints until lightly browned all over. Drain and put on one side. Reheat the margarine remaining in pan and fry the onion, carrots and bacon for 2 minutes. Stir in the flour and cook for a few minutes. Gradually pour in the wine and stock and bring to the boil stirring all the time. Add the French mustard, the bouquet garni, a little salt and plenty of freshly ground black pepper. Return the rabbit joints to the pan and bring back to the boil. Cover, reduce heat and simmer for about 1 hour, over a low heat. Add more stock if necessary. Remove rabbit joints from pan and cut flesh away from bones. Place meat in a 900ml (1½ pint) pie dish. Pour on about 150ml (¼ pint) sauce and retain remainder. Add the cooked vegetables and stir in parsley, taste and adjust seasoning. Allow to cool. Top the pie with the puff pastry, flute edges and use pastry trimmings to make leaves for decoration. Brush with a little beaten egg, bake in a hot oven for about 20 minutes. Reduce heat for a further 10 minutes. Bring remainder of sauce to boil and serve separately.

Baked gammon with marmalade and ginger

Metric

1–1¼kg lean gammon joint
1 onion, peeled and sliced
1 carrot, peeled and sliced
Bouquet garni
3–4 × 15ml spoons orange marmalade
241ml bottle ginger ale
1 × 15ml spoon cornflour
1 × 15ml spoon medium sweet sherry (optional)
Salt and freshly ground black pepper

To finish:
1 × 198g can baby carrots

Imperial

2¼–2½lb lean gammon joint
1 onion, peeled and sliced
1 carrot, peeled and sliced
Bouquet garni
3–4 tablespoons orange marmalade
8½ fl. oz bottle ginger ale
1 tablespoon cornflour
1 tablespoon medium sweet sherry (optional)
Salt and freshly ground black pepper

To finish:
1 × 7oz can baby carrots

Cooking Time: 1½–2 hours
Oven: 180°C, 350°F, Gas Mark 4

Soak the gammon in cold water for 1 hour. Drain and place in a large pan, cover with fresh cold water. Add an onion, carrot and bouquet garni. Allow 30 minutes per ½kg (1lb) weight and simmer covered for half the cooking time. Remove the gammon from the pan and peel off the skin. Line a roasting tin with enough foil to wrap round gammon and place the joint on the foil. Spread the marmalade over the fat and pour the ginger ale over. Loosely package foil around the joint and bake in a moderate oven for the rest of the calculated cooking time, basting joint frequently with the ginger ale. Transfer joint to a serving dish. Remove foil. Blend cornflour with a little cold water and stir into juices in pan with the sherry. Bring to the boil stirring all the time. Taste and adjust seasoning. Pour into a sauce boat. Serve with buttered carrots.

Gammon rashers with raisin sauce

Metric

4 gammon rashers, rinded and edges snipped at 1cm intervals
25g butter
For the sauce:
50g stoned raisins, washed
2 cloves
25g brown sugar
300ml water
3 × 5ml spoons cornflour
Cold water for blending
25g butter
Salt and freshly ground black pepper
2 × 15ml spoons lemon juice

To finish:
Lemon wedges

Imperial

4 gammon rashers, rinded and edges snipped at ½in intervals
1oz butter
For the sauce:
2oz stoned raisins, washed
2 cloves
1oz brown sugar
½ pint water
3 teaspoons cornflour
Cold water for blending
1oz butter
Salt and freshly ground black pepper
2 tablespoons lemon juice

To finish:
Lemon wedges

Cooking Time: 20 minutes

Place gammon rashers on grill grid. Heat butter and pour over rashers. Grill for 5 minutes on each side. For the sauce, place the raisins, cloves, sugar and water in a pan and bring to the boil. Simmer for 10 minutes. Remove cloves. Blend cornflour with a little cold water and stir into the raisin liquid with the butter, salt and pepper and lemon juice. Bring to the boil, stirring until thickened. Place grilled gammon rashers on a serving dish and pour over some of the raisin sauce. Serve the rest in a sauce boat. Garnish with lemon wedges.

Bacon chops in cider

Metric	Imperial
4 bacon chops, trimmed of excess fat	4 bacon chops, trimmed of excess fat
Black pepper	Black pepper
25g margarine	1oz margarine
1 small onion, peeled and finely chopped	1 small onion, peeled and finely chopped
150ml dry cider	¼ pint dry cider
1 × 5ml spoon sugar	1 teaspoon sugar
Finely grated rind of ½ orange	Finely grated rind of ½ orange
2 × 15ml spoons orange juice	2 tablespoons orange juice
1 × 5ml spoon cornflour	1 teaspoon cornflour

To finish:
Orange slices

To finish:
Orange slices

Cooking Time: 35 minutes

Soak chops in cold water for a couple of hours. Drain. Season chops with freshly ground black pepper. Heat margarine and fry chops on both sides until lightly browned. Remove from the pan and leave on one side. Fry onion until soft, add cider to the pan, with the sugar, orange rind and juice. Return chops to the pan, bring to the boil, cover and reduce heat. Allow to simmer gently for 30 minutes. Blend cornflour with a little cold water, stir into cider liquid and bring to the boil, stirring. Taste and adjust seasoning. Place chops on a serving dish, spoon sauce over, garnish with orange slices and serve with savoury rice.

Gammon rashers with raisin sauce; Baked gammon with marmalade and ginger; Bacon chops in cider

Pear and orange tart

Metric	Imperial
Rich shortcrust pastry, made with 225g plain flour, 150g fat, and 2–3 × 15ml spoons cold water	Rich shortcrust pastry, made with 8oz plain flour, 6oz fat, and 2–3 tablespoons cold water
411g can pear halves, drained	14½oz can pear halves, drained
Finely grated rind and juice of ½ orange	Finely grated rind and juice of ½ orange
Egg white, beaten for glazing	Egg white, beaten for glazing
Caster sugar for sprinkling	Caster sugar for sprinkling
To finish:	To finish:
150ml whipping cream	¼ pint whipping cream

Cooking Time: 35 minutes
Oven: 190°C, 375°F, Gas Mark 5

Line a 20cm (8in) plain flan ring with half the pastry. Prick the base with a fork. Arrange the pear halves in the flan ring, sprinkle the orange rind over the fruit and pour over the orange juice. Roll out a lid using the rest of the pastry and cut away a circle in the centre of the lid, using a 7.5cm (3in) plain cutter. Carefully lift the pastry over the pears and top the tart, sealing the edges well. Brush with egg white and sprinkle sugar over the surface. Cook in a moderately hot oven for about 35 minutes until pastry is lightly browned. Allow to cool, remove tart from the flan ring onto a serving plate. Lightly whip the cream and spoon some into the central space. Serve the rest in a jug.

Latticed blackcurrant flan

Metric	Imperial
150g plain flour	6oz plain flour
50g margarine	2oz margarine
50g lard	2oz lard
2 × 15ml spoons cold water	2 tablespoons cold water
1 egg, beaten	1 egg, beaten
142g carton soured cream	5oz carton soured cream
389g can blackcurrant pie filling	13¾oz can blackcurrant pie filling

Cooking Time: 30 minutes
Oven: 220°C, 425°F, Gas Mark 7
Reduce to: 180°C, 350°F, Gas Mark 4

Rub fats into flour and mix to a firm dough with cold water. Roll out and line a 20cm (8in) fluted flan ring placed on a baking sheet. Prick base and sides with a fork. Brush with a little beaten egg. Chill in the refrigerator for 10 minutes. Spread the soured cream over the base of the flan and spoon the pie filling over the cream. Roll out the pastry trimmings, cut into strips using a pastry wheel and use to make a lattice design over flan. Brush pastry with beaten egg and bake in a hot oven for 15 minutes, and reduce the oven temperature for a further 15 minutes. Serve hot or cold.

Apple and raisin plate tart

Metric	Imperial
Shortcrust pastry made with 200g plain flour, 100g fat, and 2–3 × 15ml spoons cold water	Shortcrust pastry made with 8oz plain flour, 4oz fat, and 2–3 tablespoons cold water
450g cooking apples, peeled, cored and sliced	1lb cooking apples, peeled, cored and sliced
75g seedless raisins	3oz seedless raisins
25g sugar	1oz sugar
1 × 5ml spoon powdered cinnamon	1 teaspoon powdered cinnamon
Milk for brushing	Milk for brushing
Sugar for sprinkling	Sugar for sprinkling

Cooking Time: 30 minutes
Oven: 200°C, 400°F, Gas Mark 6

Divide the pastry in half and roll out one half to line the base of the 20cm (8in) plate. Put the apples in a basin, add the raisins and sprinkle over sugar and cinnamon. Mix well and spoon the apple mixture onto the pastry-lined plate. Dampen the edges and roll out the remaining pastry to form a lid. Seal edges well, flute and make a slit in the centre. Brush with milk and dredge with a little sugar. Leave in refrigerator for 10 minutes, cook in a hot oven for about 35 minutes until pastry is well coloured. Serve with ice-cream or custard.

To freeze: Wrap tart, cooked and cooled, or uncooked, in a plastic bag. Remove air, seal, label and freeze. Bake from frozen for about 45 minutes at 200°C, 400°F, Gas Mark 6.

Latticed blackcurrant flan; Pear and orange tart; Apple and raisin plate tart

Mincemeat and apricot plait

Metric	Imperial
225g bought puff pastry	8oz bought puff pastry
175g mincemeat	6oz mincemeat
439g can apricots, drained	15oz can apricots, drained
Beaten egg for glazing	Beaten egg for glazing

Cooking Time: 20 minutes
Oven: 220°C, 425°F, Gas Mark 7

Roll out the pastry to an oblong 22.5cm × 33cm (9in × 13in). Place on a baking sheet. Roughly mark the pastry into three sections, lengthwise, and spread the mincemeat down the centre section. Arrange the apricots over the mincemeat, make diagonal cuts 2cm ($\frac{1}{2}$in) apart along the uncovered pastry at each side, to within 1cm ($\frac{1}{4}$in) of the filling. Brush pastry strips with egg and plait over apricots. Brush outside of pastry with egg glaze and cook in a hot oven for about 20 minutes until golden. Serve hot, in slices, with whipped cream.

Syrup tart

Metric	Imperial
Shortcrust pastry, made with 150g plain flour, 75g fat, and 2 × 15ml spoons cold water	Shortcrust pastry, made with 6oz plain flour, 3oz fat, and 2 tablespoons cold water
9 × 15ml spoons golden syrup	9 tablespoons golden syrup
75g fresh white breadcrumbs	3oz fresh white breadcrumbs
Finely grated rind of 1 lemon	Finely grated rind of 1 lemon

Cooking Time: 20 minutes
Oven: 220°C, 425°F, Gas Mark 7

Line a 20cm (8in) flan ring or pie plate with the pastry. Warm the syrup in a pan and pour onto the breadcrumbs and lemon rind. Spoon breadcrumb mixture into the pastry-lined tin and cook in a hot oven for about 20 minutes. Serve hot with a custard sauce.

Rhubarb brûlée

Metric	Imperial
450g fresh rhubarb, washed and chopped	1lb fresh rhubarb, washed and chopped
2 × 5ml spoons water	2 teaspoons water
$\frac{1}{2}$ teaspoon powdered cinnamon	$\frac{1}{2}$ teaspoon powdered cinnamon
50g granulated sugar	2oz granulated sugar
142g carton soured cream	5oz carton soured cream
Soft light brown sugar	Soft light brown sugar

This is a quick, tasty sweet to impress the family. Cook rhubarb in a little water with cinnamon and sugar until soft and reduced to a pulp. Divide between four ramekin dishes. Top each one with some soured cream, sprinkle brown sugar liberally over the cream to a 1cm ($\frac{1}{4}$in) thickness and flash under a pre-heated grill until the sugar caramelises – about 2–3 minutes. Serve from the grill, or chill before serving. Other fruit can be substituted for rhubarb – peaches, apples, blackcurrants, etc.

Hot spicy fruit salad

Metric	Imperial
25g soft brown sugar	1oz soft brown sugar
600ml water	1 pint water
1 × 15ml spoon clear honey	1 tablespoon clear honey
1 × 5ml spoon powdered cinnamon	1 teaspoon powdered cinnamon
1 × 5ml spoon powdered nutmeg	1 teaspoon powdered nutmeg
2 cloves	2 cloves
2 × 15ml spoons lemon juice	2 tablespoons lemon juice
1 × 15ml spoon brandy (optional)	1 tablespoon brandy (optional)
125g dried apricots, washed	4oz dried apricots, washed
822g can peach halves, drained	1lb 13oz can peach halves, drained
50g sultanas	2oz sultanas

Cooking Time: 45 minutes

Dissolve sugar in water in a pan. Add the honey, cinnamon, nutmeg, cloves, lemon juice and brandy. Bring to the boil, then reduce heat. Add the apricots, cover, and allow to simmer for 15 minutes. Stir in the peaches and simmer for a further 30 minutes. Remove the cloves. Just before serving add the sultanas. Serve hot with lots of whipped cream.

Lemon sponge pudding

Metric	Imperial
50g margarine	2oz margarine
125g caster sugar	4oz caster sugar
Finely grated rind and juice of 2 lemons	Finely grated rind and juice of 2 lemons
2 eggs, separated	2 eggs, separated
300ml milk	½ pint milk
50g self-raising flour	2oz self-raising flour

Cooking Time: 1 hour
Oven: 180°C, 350°F, Gas Mark 4

Cream the margarine and sugar together with the lemon rind until pale and fluffy. Add the egg yolks and beat in well. Stir in half the milk, then the flour. Pour in the rest of the milk and the lemon juice. Whisk the egg whites until just holding their shape and fold into the mixture. Pour into a greased 1¼l (2 pint) ovenproof pie dish and place this in a roasting tin half filled with water. Cook in the centre of a moderate oven for about 1 hour, until a golden brown and firm to the touch. The pudding will separate out into a creamy base and sponge top, when cooked. Serve hot with custard or ice-cream.

Pear and ginger upside-down pudding

Metric	Imperial
4 × 15ml spoons golden syrup	4 tablespoons golden syrup
411g can pears, drained and juice retained	14½oz can pears, drained and juice retained
4 glacé cherries	4 glacé cherries
100g soft margarine	4oz soft margarine
100g caster sugar	4oz caster sugar
2 eggs	2 eggs
150g self-raising flour	6oz self-raising flour
2 × 5ml spoons powdered ginger	2 teaspoons powdered ginger
A little milk	A little milk
2 × 5ml spoons cornflour	2 teaspoons cornflour

Cooking Time: 45–55 minutes
Oven: 180°C, 350°F, Gas Mark 4

This is a popular favourite with the family. Grease a 20cm (8in) round cake tin. Heat the syrup and pour into the tin and cover the base. Arrange the pears and glacé cherries in the syrup. Cream the fat and sugar together until light and fluffy. Beat in the eggs and finally stir in the sieved flour and ginger. Add a little milk to give a dropping consistency. Spread the mixture over the fruit and cook in a moderate oven for about 45–55 minutes until golden brown and firm to the touch. Turn out onto a serving dish and serve with a pear sauce made by blending the cornflour with a little juice and heating with the rest of the juice to boiling point, stirring all the time.

Christmas pudding

Metric

150g plain flour
1 × 5ml spoon grated nutmeg
1 × 5ml spoon powdered mace
100g beef suet, shredded
200g currants, washed
150g sultanas, washed
150g stoned raisins, chopped
75g brown sugar
Finely grated rind of 1 lemon
1 carrot, peeled and grated
75g fresh white breadcrumbs
2 standard eggs, beaten
150ml brown ale

Imperial

6oz plain flour
1 teaspoon grated nutmeg
1 teaspoon powdered mace
4oz beef suet, shredded
8oz currants, washed
6oz sultanas, washed
6oz stoned raisins, chopped
3oz brown sugar
Finely grated rind of 1 lemon
1 carrot, peeled and grated
3oz fresh white breadcrumbs
2 large eggs, beaten
⅓ pint brown ale

Cooking Time: 6 hours + 3 hours

Grease a 1.2l (2 pint) pudding basin. Sieve the flour and spices and add the suet, dried fruit, sugar, lemon rind, carrot and breadcrumbs. Mix well together and bind together with eggs and brown ale. Spoon the mixture into the prepared basin, cover with greased greaseproof paper, and aluminium foil. Place in a steamer or large saucepan, half filled with water and simmer covered for 6 hours, or steam for 8 hours. Keep up the water level with boiling water. Remove, allow to cool and store in a cool place. On Christmas Day re-boil for 3 hours. Serve with brandy sauce.

Apple and almond pancakes

Metric

125g flour
Pinch salt
1 standard egg
300ml milk
Oil for frying pancakes
2 × 15ml spoons single cream
½kg apple purée or 398g can apple pie filling
Few drops almond essence
25g sugar (optional)
25g ground almonds
50g butter
25g flaked almonds

Imperial

4oz flour
Pinch salt
1 standard egg
½ pint milk
Oil for frying pancakes
2 tablespoons single cream
1lb apple purée or 13¾oz can apple pie filling
Few drops almond essence
1oz sugar (optional)
1oz ground almonds
2oz butter
1oz flaked almonds

Cooking Time: 20 minutes
Oven: 190°C, 375°F, Gas Mark 5

The pancakes can be made a day ahead and stored, wrapped, in the refrigerator. Sieve flour and salt in a bowl, make a well in the centre and add the egg with half the milk. Beat until smooth. Stir in the rest of the milk. Use to make six 20cm (8in) pancakes. Stir cream into the apple purée with the almond essence and sugar, (if used). Place a pancake on the base of an ovenproof plate or dish, spread some apple mixture over and sprinkle some ground almonds on top. Continue to layer pancakes, apple filling and almonds ending with a pancake. Heat butter over a low heat and pour over pancakes. Sprinkle the flaked almonds on top and cook in a moderately hot oven for about 20 minutes. Serve hot, cut into segments, with whipped cream.

Baked alaska

Metric

1 × 22cm bought sponge flan case
483g block vanilla ice-cream
382g can blackberries, drained
3 egg whites
150g caster sugar

Imperial

1 × 9in bought sponge flan case
17fl.oz block vanilla ice-cream
13½oz can blackberries, drained
3 egg whites
6oz caster sugar

Cooking Time: 5 minutes
Oven: 220°C, 425°F, Gas Mark 7

Place the sponge flan case on a heatproof serving dish. Place the block of ice-cream in the sponge flan case. Spoon the blackberries over the ice-cream. Whisk the egg whites until stiff. Beat in the sugar a little at a time until all is incorporated. Cover ice-cream and sponge base with the meringue and bake in a hot oven for 5 minutes. Serve immediately.

Apple and almond pancakes; Baked alaska; Christmas pudding

Strawberry mousse

Metric	Imperial
225g fresh or frozen strawberries, thawed	8oz fresh or frozen strawberries, thawed
3 egg yolks	3 egg yolks
25g caster sugar	1oz caster sugar
150ml whipping or double cream	¼ pint whipping or double cream
2 egg whites	2 egg whites
Red colouring (optional)	Red colouring (optional)

To finish:
Toasted flaked almonds

To finish:
Toasted flaked almonds

This is ideal to make using over-ripe strawberries. Sieve the strawberries. Whisk the egg yolks, sugar and strawberry purée over hot water until thick. Remove from the heat and whisk until cold. Lightly whip the cream, fold into the strawberry mixture. Lightly whisk the egg whites and fold these in. Add a little red colouring if liked. Spoon into a large serving bowl or individual sundae glasses. Chill. Decorate with toasted flaked almonds. This pudding is best eaten the day it is made.

Baked cheese cake

Metric	Imperial
100g butter	4oz butter
225g ginger nut biscuits, finely crushed	8oz ginger nut biscuits, finely crushed
225g curd cheese	8oz curd cheese
25g caster sugar	1oz caster sugar
1 egg beaten	1 egg, beaten
150ml whipping cream, lightly whipped	¼ pint whipping cream, lightly whipped
Finely grated rind of 1 lemon	Finely grated rind of 1 lemon
40g sultanas	1½oz sultanas

To finish:
150ml whipping cream, lightly whipped
Lemon butterflies

To finish:
¼ pint whipping cream, lightly whipped
Lemon butterflies

Cooking Time: 30 minutes
Oven: 180°C, 350°F, Gas Mark 4

Melt butter in a pan and stir into biscuit crumbs. Mix well together and use to line a 22cm (9in) ovenproof pie plate or a loose bottomed flan case. Put in the refrigerator for 10 minutes. Beat the cheese with the sugar until soft. Gradually beat in the egg and finally the cream and lemon rind. Stir in the sultanas. Spoon the mixture into the biscuit crust and bake in a moderate oven for about 30 minutes. Cool. Remove flan ring, if used, and serve cold in wedges decorated with whipped cream and lemon slices. This stores well for a few days in the refrigerator.

Country cream

Metric	Imperial
500ml milk	1 pint milk
25–50g sugar	1–2oz sugar
4 eggs, beaten	4 eggs, beaten

To finish:
3 × 15ml spoons raspberry or apricot jam
200ml whipping cream
25g dark cooking chocolate, grated

To finish:
3 tablespoons raspberry or apricot jam
⅓ pint whipping cream
1oz dark cooking chocolate, grated

Cooking Time: 1½ hours
Oven: 160°C, 325°F, Gas Mark 3

A delicious way of serving a baked custard to please all the family. Heat the milk with the sugar and pour onto the eggs. Strain the mixture into a 1¼l (2 pint) ovenproof dish. Cover with foil and stand in a baking tin with a little water. Bake in a slow oven for 1¼–1½ hours until set. Cool the custard and spread jam over the surface. Lightly whip the cream and spoon over the layer of jam. Top with grated chocolate. Serve chilled.

Gooseberry fool

Metric

552g can gooseberries, drained and 3 × 15ml spoons of juice retained
150ml cold custard made with 1 × 15ml spoon custard powder, 15g sugar and 150ml milk
142g carton natural yoghurt
Few drops green colouring

To finish:
25g plain chocolate, grated

Imperial

1lb 3½oz can gooseberries, drained and retain 3 tablespoons of juice
¼ pint cold custard made with 1 tablespoon custard powder, ½ tablespoon sugar and ¼ pint milk
5oz carton natural yoghurt
Few drops green colouring

To finish:
1oz plain chocolate, grated

Purée the canned fruit to a cream in an electric blender, or through a sieve, adding juice to the fruit. Pour into a bowl and beat in the cold custard and yoghurt. Stir in green colouring and pour into individual glass dishes. Decorate with grated chocolate and serve shortbread biscuits separately.

N.B. If using fresh fruit, top and tail the gooseberries, wash, then simmer with a little water and sugar to taste until soft. Pass through a sieve or purée in an electric blender, then follow recipe as above.

Apples and oranges bristol

Metric

75g granulated sugar
300ml water
4 dessert apples, peeled, cored and thickly sliced
½ teaspoon vanilla essence
3 large oranges

For caramel topping:
100g granulated sugar
150ml water

Imperial

3oz granulated sugar
½ pint water
4 dessert apples, peeled, cored and thickly sliced
½ teaspoon vanilla essence
3 large oranges

For caramel topping:
4oz granulated sugar
¼ pint water

Cooking Time: approx. 10 minutes

Dissolve the sugar slowly in the water, then boil rapidly for 1 minute. Add the apples and vanilla essence and simmer for about 5 minutes, until fruit is tender. Remove from heat and leave covered, until cold. Pare the rind from 1 orange, cut into thin strips and boil for 5 minutes. Drain well. Remove the peel and pith from the oranges, slice into rounds. Dissolve sugar for caramel in water until it caramelises. Pour onto an oiled baking tin and leave to harden. Crack with a rolling pin. Spoon the apples carefully into a serving bowl with the syrup, arrange the oranges on top and sprinkle the orange peel and cracked caramel pieces over. Serve chilled.

Chocolate mousse

Metric

175g plain cooking chocolate
25g butter
3 eggs, separated

To finish:
4 × 15ml spoons whipping or double cream, lightly whipped
Chopped nuts

Imperial

6oz plain cooking chocolate
1oz butter
3 eggs, separated

To finish:
4 tablespoons whipping or double cream, lightly whipped
Chopped nuts

Heat chocolate pieces in a bowl over a pan of hot water. Off the heat, beat in butter and egg yolks. Lightly whisk the egg whites until just holding shape and fold into the chocolate mixture. Spoon into ramekin dishes and decorate with a whirl of cream and a few chopped nuts.

Chocolate mousse; Gooseberry fool; Apples and oranges bristol

Lemon crunch flan

Metric

75g butter
175g digestive biscuits,
crushed
150ml double cream
Small can condensed milk
Finely grated rind of 1
lemon
6 × 15ml spoons lemon
  juice

To finish:
2 digestive biscuits,
crushed

Imperial

3oz butter
6oz digestive biscuits,
crushed
¼ pint double cream
Small can condensed milk
Finely grated rind of 1
lemon
6 tablespoons lemon
juice

To finish:
2 digestive biscuits,
crushed

Melt the butter and stir into the crushed biscuits in a bowl.
Mix well and use to line a 20cm (8in) pie plate or flan ring,
placed on a baking sheet. Place in the refrigerator for 10
minutes. Lightly whip the cream and stir in the condensed
milk, lemon rind and juice. Beat until thoroughly blended.
Pour into the prepared biscuit case and chill in the refrigerator until set. Decorate with biscuit crumbs in a lattice
design.

Lemon crunch flán; Gooseberry cheesecake; Strawberry topped pavlova

Strawberry topped pavlova

Metric	Imperial
4 egg whites	4 egg whites
225g caster sugar	8oz caster sugar
½ teaspoon vanilla essence	½ teaspoon vanilla essence
1 × 5ml spoon vinegar	1 teaspoon vinegar
1 × 5ml spoon cornflour	1 teaspoon cornflour
300ml double or whipping cream	½ pint double or whipping cream
225g fresh strawberries, washed and hulled, or	8oz fresh strawberries, washed and hulled, or
426g can strawberries, drained	15oz can strawberries, drained

Cooking Time: 1 hour
Oven: 120°C, 250°F, Gas Mark ½

The soft marshmallow-like texture of this meringue is a pleasant change. Draw a 20cm (8in) circle on non-stick paper and place on a baking sheet. Whisk the egg whites until stiff and standing in peaks, beat in the sugar, 1 × 15ml spoon (1 tablespoon) at a time. Beat in the vanilla essence, vinegar and cornflour. Spoon the meringue mixture over the round, making a slight hollow in the centre. Cook in a slow oven for about 1 hour, until firm. Leave to cool, then remove the paper. Place on a serving plate. Lightly whip the cream and pile into the hollow and top with strawberries. The meringue case will crack slightly on cooling.

Gooseberry cheesecake

Metric	Imperial
450 g fresh or frozen gooseberries, thawed	1 lb fresh or frozen gooseberries, thawed
75 g sugar	3 oz sugar
3 × 5 ml spoons powdered gelatine	3 teaspoons powdered gelatine
2 × 15 ml spoons water	2 tablespoons water
225 g cream cheese	8 oz cream cheese
150 ml double cream, lightly whipped	¼ pint double cream, lightly whipped
100 g ginger biscuits, crushed	4 oz ginger biscuits, crushed

Lightly grease the base of a 18 cm (7 inch) round loose-bottomed cake tin. Cook gooseberries with the sugar for 15 minutes until soft, then sieve. Sprinkle gelatine over water in a basin, place over a pan of hot water, and dissolve. Add the gelatine to the gooseberry purée. Lightly beat the cream cheese and stir in the cream and gooseberry purée mixture. Pour the mixture into the tin and leave to set. Sprinkle biscuit crumbs over surface and, if liked, decorate with whole gooseberries.
To freeze: Open freeze in the tin, cover with foil, label and freeze. To thaw, place in the refrigerator for about 8 hours. Turn out onto a serving dish.

Vanilla ice-cream

Metric	Imperial
2 × 15ml spoons cornflour	2 tablespoons cornflour
150ml water	¼ pint water
Large can of evaporated milk, well chilled in refrigerator	Large can of evaporated milk, well chilled in refrigerator
25g sugar	1oz sugar
½ teaspoon vanilla essence	½ teaspoon vanilla essence

Cooking Time: 7–10 minutes

Turn freezing compartment switch on refrigerator to the coldest setting. Blend cornflour with a little of the water. Stir in half the can of evaporated milk (returning the remainder to the refrigerator until needed). Add the rest of the water and sugar. Bring to the boil, stirring, until thickened. Cook for a further 2 minutes. Allow to cool quickly. Chill, covered in the refrigerator. Whisk the remaining chilled evaporated milk until thick. Beat in the chilled cornflour sauce until smooth. Add vanilla essence. Pour into ice-cube trays or a 450g (1lb) loaf tin. Put to freeze. After 30 minutes remove and stir mixture thoroughly. Return to freezer until frozen. Serve with wafer biscuits and one of the following sauces.

Melba sauce

Metric	Imperial
225g fresh raspberries or frozen, thawed	8oz fresh raspberries or frozen, thawed
3 × 15ml spoons icing sugar, sieved	3 tablespoons icing sugar, sieved

Rub raspberries through a sieve and beat icing sugar into fruit purée, a little at a time until it thickens.

Chocolate sauce

Metric	Imperial
50g cooking chocolate	2oz cooking chocolate
15g cocoa	½oz cocoa
300ml water	½ pint water
2 × 15ml spoons sugar	2 tablespoons sugar

Cooking Time: 10–15 minutes

Put all the ingredients into a saucepan. Bring to the boil and boil rapidly until of a pouring consistency – about 10 minutes. This sauce stores well in a screw-topped jar in the refrigerator for a fortnight.

Honey, orange and raisin sauce

Metric	Imperial
50g butter	2oz butter
1 × 15ml spoon cornflour	1 tablespoon cornflour
100g honey	4oz honey
2 × 15ml spoons fresh orange juice	2 tablespoons fresh orange juice
1 × 5ml spoon lemon juice	1 tablespoon lemon juice
3 × 15ml spoons warm water	3 tablespoons warm water
25g stoned raisins, washed	1oz stoned raisins, washed

Cooking Time: 7–10 minutes

Heat butter and stir in cornflour and cook for a few minutes. Off the heat slowly add the honey, orange and lemon juice and water. Return to the heat and bring to the boil stirring. Add the raisins and serve hot.

Vanilla ice-cream with: Melba sauce; Honey, orange and raisin sauce; Chocolate sauce

Tagliatelle in seafood sauce

Metric	Imperial
100g tagliatelle verdi	4oz tagliatelle verdi
Knob of butter	Knob of butter
300ml white coating sauce made with 25g flour, 25g margarine and 300ml milk	½ pint white coating sauce made with 1oz flour, 1oz margarine and ½ pint milk
198g can shrimps, drained or 100g frozen shrimps, thawed	7oz can shrimps, drained or 4oz frozen shrimps, thawed
½ red pepper, seeded and thinly sliced	½ red pepper, seeded and thinly sliced
Salt and freshly ground black pepper	Salt and freshly ground black pepper
Parmesan cheese, finely grated	Parmesan cheese, finely grated

Cooking Time: 12–15 minutes

Cook tagliatelle in boiling, salted water for 7 minutes. Drain well and toss with butter. Simmer the white sauce and stir in the shrimps and red pepper for 5 minutes. Season well. Pile the tagliatelle on a heated dish, pour the shrimp and pepper sauce over. Sprinkle with Parmesan cheese and serve more separately.

Lasagne

Metric	Imperial
25g margarine	1oz margarine
1 large onion, peeled and sliced	1 large onion, peeled and sliced
250g minced beef	8oz minced beef
396g can tomatoes	14oz can tomatoes
2 × 5ml spoons tomato purée	2 teaspoons tomato purée
150ml beef stock	¼ pint beef stock
1 × 5ml spoon dried marjoram	1 teaspoon dried marjoram
1 × 5ml spoon dried basil	1 teaspoon dried basil
1 clove of garlic, peeled and crushed (optional)	1 clove of garlic, peeled and crushed (optional)
Salt and freshly ground black pepper	Salt and freshly ground black pepper
2 × 5ml spoons cornflour	2 teaspoons cornflour
150g lasagne	6oz lasagne
25g margarine	1oz margarine
25g flour	1oz flour
300ml milk	½ pint milk
65g Cheddar cheese, grated	2½oz Cheddar cheese, grated

Cooking Time: 35 minutes
Oven: 190°C, 375°F, Gas Mark 5

Heat the margarine and fry the onion until soft. Stir in the minced beef and cook until lightly browned. Add the tomatoes, tomato purée, stock, herbs and garlic. Season well, cover and simmer for 30 minutes. Blend cornflour with cold water and stir into meat sauce. Bring to the boil stirring. Cook the lasagne in boiling, salted water for 10–15 minutes. Drain carefully and refresh in cold water. For coating sauce, heat the margarine and stir in the flour and cook for a few minutes. Allow to cool, then slowly add milk. Return to the heat and bring to the boil stirring constantly. Stir in half the cheese. Cover the base of an oiled ovenproof dish with half the lasagne. Spoon over half the tomato and meat sauce, top with the rest of the pasta and spoon over the remaining meat sauce. Pour on the cheese sauce, sprinkle rest of cheese on top and cook in a moderately hot oven for about 30–35 minutes. Serve hot with a tomato salad.

Pizza neopolitan

Metric	Imperial
225g strong plain flour	8oz strong plain flour
½ teaspoon salt	½ teaspoon salt
25g lard	1oz lard
15g fresh yeast (or 7g dried yeast – see note)	½oz fresh yeast (or ¼oz dried yeast – see note)
150ml tepid water	¼ pint tepid water
2 × 15ml spoons oil	2 tablespoons oil
25g margarine	1oz margarine
2 onions, peeled and sliced	2 onions, peeled and sliced
396g can tomatoes, drained and halved	14oz can tomatoes, drained and halved
1 × 5ml spoon dried marjoram	1 teaspoon dried marjoram
100g Cheddar cheese, coarsely grated	4oz Cheddar cheese, coarsely grated
Salt and freshly ground black pepper	Salt and freshly ground black pepper
56g can anchovy fillets, drained	2oz can anchovy fillets, drained
6 black olives, halved and stoned	6 black olives, halved and stoned

Cooking Time: 25 minutes
Oven: 220°C, 425°F, Gas Mark 7

The dough can be made the previous evening and left to rise in the refrigerator. Sieve flour in a bowl and stir in salt. Rub fat into flour. Blend fresh yeast with the tepid water and add to the flour. Mix to form a firm dough. Knead well for 10 minutes on a floured board. Place in an oiled plastic bag and leave to rise at room temperature for an hour (or 40 minutes in a warm place, or overnight in the refrigerator). Knock back dough and roll large enough to cover the base of a 28cm (11in) flan tin. Brush surface with oil, heat margarine and cook onions until soft. Top dough with these and spoon over the tomatoes. Stir herbs into cheese and sprinkle this over the tomatoes. Season well. Arrange the anchovies in a lattice and place the olives in the squares. Bake in a hot oven for about 25 minutes. Serve hot with a tossed green salad.

N.B. Reconstitute the dried yeast by sprinkling it over warm water with 5ml (1 teaspoon) sugar, mixing with a fork. Leave until frothy (about 20 minutes) and add to flour and proceed as above.

Pasta and pork au gratin

Metric	Imperial
25g butter	1oz butter
1 large onion, peeled and thinly sliced	1 large onion, peeled and thinly sliced
350g lean minced pork	12oz lean minced pork
396g can tomatoes	14oz can tomatoes
1 × 15ml spoon medium dry sherry	1 tablespoon medium dry sherry
1 clove of garlic, peeled and crushed	1 clove of garlic, peeled and crushed
½ teaspoon dried thyme	½ teaspoon dried thyme
1 bay leaf	1 bay leaf
Salt and freshly ground black pepper	Salt and freshly ground black pepper
454g packet frozen whole leaf spinach	1lb packet frozen whole leaf spinach
2 knobs of butter	2 knobs of butter
150g noodles	6oz noodles
2 × 5ml spoons cornflour	2 teaspoons cornflour
450ml cheese sauce (see recipe for Cauliflower au Gratin, page 20)	¾ pint cheese sauce (see recipe for Cauliflower au Gratin, page 20)
To finish:	To finish:
50g Cheddar cheese, coarsely grated	2oz Cheddar cheese, coarsely grated

Cooking Time: 30 minutes
Oven: 180°C, 350°F, Gas Mark 4

Heat butter and fry onion until soft. Gradually add the pork and cook until lightly browned. Stir in the tomatoes, add sherry, garlic, thyme and bay leaf. Season well and allow to simmer covered for 30 minutes. Heat frozen spinach with a knob of butter. When soft drain well and spread over base of a greased ovenproof dish. Cook noodles in plenty of boiling, salted water for 5 minutes. Drain and add a knob of butter. Blend cornflour with a little cold water, stir into pork and tomato mixture and bring to the boil. Taste and adjust seasoning. Spoon half the cheese sauce over the spinach, top with buttered noodles, then the meat sauce and finally pour over remaining cheese sauce. Sprinkle with the grated cheese and bake in a hot oven for 30 minutes. Serve with a salad.

Mushroom and bacon quiche

Metric	Imperial
Shortcrust pastry made with 175g plain flour, 100g fat and 2 × 15ml spoons cold water	Short crust pastry made with 6oz plain flour, 4oz fat and 2 tablespoons cold water
15g butter	½oz butter
1 rasher streaky bacon, rinded and chopped	1 rasher streaky bacon, rinded and chopped
100g button mushrooms, washed and sliced	4oz button mushrooms, washed and sliced
2 large eggs	2 large eggs
165ml milk	⅓ pint milk
Salt and freshly ground black pepper	Salt and freshly ground black pepper
To finish:	To finish:
Chopped parsley	Chopped parsley

Cooking Time: 50 minutes
Oven: 200°C, 400°F, Gas Mark 6
Reduce to: 180°C, 350°F, Gas Mark 4

Good results in pastry making are achieved by keeping utensils, hands and ingredients as cool as possible. Make shortcrust pastry by sieving the flour into a bowl, then rub in the fat until mixture resembles fine breadcrumbs. Add water and mix to form a pliable dough. Allow a pastry to rest for at least 15 minutes in a refrigerator before use. Roll out pastry and use to line a 20cm (8in) flan ring set on a baking tray. Place in the refrigerator to chill for 15 minutes. Melt the butter in a saucepan, add the prepared bacon and mushrooms and cook for 2 minutes. Drain on kitchen paper. Beat together the eggs, milk and seasoning. Line the prepared flan ring with foil or greaseproof paper, add baking beans and bake blind at the top of a hot oven for 10 minutes. Remove foil, or greaseproof paper and beans, and cook for a further 10 minutes at the same temperature. Fill the baked flan with the mushroom and bacon, pour the seasoned savoury custard over and bake at the same temperature for 10 minutes. Then turn oven down to 180°C, 350°F, Gas Mark 4 for a further 20 minutes. Garnish with chopped parsley and serve with buttered French beans.
Shortcrust pastry can be made with half fat to flour and the fat can be a mixture of whitefat and margarine. A slightly richer pastry can be made by increasing the proportion of fat to flour.

Chicken flan

Metric	Imperial
175g cooked chicken	6oz cooked chicken
25g margarine	1oz margarine
25g flour	1oz flour
300ml milk	½ pint milk
Salt and freshly ground black pepper	Salt and freshly ground black pepper
1 × 15ml spoon finely chopped parsley	1 tablespoon finely chopped parsley
Finely grated rind of ½ lemon	Finely grated rind of ½ lemon
20cm baked flan case	8in baked flan case

Cooking Time: 30 minutes
Oven: 180°C, 350°F, Gas Mark 4

This is a tasty way to use up cold chicken or turkey for a supper or high tea dish. Cut chicken into bite-size pieces. Make a white coating sauce (see recipe for Cauliflower au Gratin, page 20), season well with salt and ground black pepper. Add parsley and lemon rind to sauce. Stir in the prepared chicken and spoon mixture into the baked flan case, placed on a baking sheet. Cook in a moderate oven for 30 minutes. Serve hot with boiled potatoes and a tossed green salad.

Sausage and tomato quiche

Metric	Imperial
225g chipolata sausages	8oz chipolata sausages
Shortcrust pastry made with 175g plain flour, 100g fat, and 2 × 15ml spoons cold water	Shortcrust pastry made with 6oz plain flour, 4oz fat, and 2 tablespoons cold water
75g Cheddar cheese, coarsely grated	3oz Cheddar cheese, coarsely grated
2 tomatoes, skinned and sliced	2 tomatoes, skinned and sliced
2 eggs	2 eggs
190ml milk	⅓ pint milk
½ teaspoon dried basil	½ teaspoon dried basil
Salt and freshly ground black pepper	Salt and freshly ground black pepper

Cooking Time: 50 minutes
Oven: 200°C, 400°F, Gas Mark 6
Reduce to: 180°C, 350°F, Gas Mark 4

Grill sausages until lightly browned. Line a 23cm (9 in) flan case or pie plate with the pastry. Prick the base and sides with a fork and bake blind for 20 minutes in a hot oven. Sprinkle the cheese over the base of the cooked pastry case. Arrange the cooked sausages in a wheel design, put tomato slices in the spaces. Beat eggs, stir in milk, add basil and season. Pour savoury custard over filling. Turn oven down and bake for 30–35 minutes. Serve hot or cold with a rice salad.

Chicken flan; Sausage and tomato quiche; Mushroom and bacon quiche

Bacon and egg pie

Metric	*Imperial*
Shortcrust pastry made with 225g flour, 125g fat, and 2–3 × 15ml spoons cold water	*Shortcrust pastry made with 8oz flour, 5oz fat, and 2–3 tablespoons cold water*
4 rashers bacon, rinded and chopped	*4 rashers bacon, rinded and chopped*
50g mushrooms, washed and sliced	*2oz mushrooms, washed and sliced*
4 large eggs	*4 large eggs*
5 × 15ml spoons milk	*5 tablespoons milk*
Salt and freshly ground black pepper	*Salt and freshly ground black pepper*
1 × 5ml spoon dried thyme	*1 teaspoon dried thyme*
1 × 15ml spoon chopped parsley	*1 tablespoon chopped parsley*
2 tomatoes, sliced	*2 tomatoes, sliced*

Cooking Time: 40 minutes
Oven: 200°C, 400°F, Gas Mark 6
Reduce to: 180°C, 350°F, Gas Mark 4

Roll out half pastry and use to line a 20cm (8in) sandwich tin. Roll out the remaining pastry to form a lid. Put bacon over the base and top with mushrooms. Whisk the eggs together and stir in the milk. Season well, and add the thyme and parsley. Pour over the bacon and mushroom mixture, top with tomato slices. Damp the edges of the pastry and cover with the lid, sealing well together. Trim and scallop edges and make pastry leaves with left over pastry, and use to decorate centre of pastry top. Brush with egg left over in the basin and cook in a hot oven for 10 minutes, reducing the oven temperature for the next 30 minutes. Serve hot with buttered noodles and peas, or cold with a salad.

Kipper and cheese flan

Metric	*Imperial*
Shortcrust pastry made with 175g plain flour, 100g fat, and 2 × 15ml spoons cold water	*Shortcrust pastry made with 6oz plain flour, 4oz fat, and 2 tablespoons cold water*
175g kipper fillets	*6oz kipper fillets*
2 eggs	*2 eggs*
180ml milk	*6fl.oz milk*
40g coarsely grated Cheddar cheese	*1½oz coarsely grated Cheddar cheese*
Salt and freshly ground black pepper	*Salt and freshly ground black pepper*

Cooking Time: 30 minutes
Oven: 200°C, 400°F, Gas Mark 6
Reduce to: 180°C, 350°F, Gas Mark 4

Line a 22cm (9in) flan ring with the pastry. Bake pastry case blind in a hot oven for 20 minutes. (See recipe for Mushroom and Bacon Quiche, page 79, for instructions on baking blind.) Poach kipper fillets for 6–8 minutes. Drain and remove skins. Beat eggs, stir in milk and grated cheese. Season well. Arrange kipper fillets in pastry case and pour over the cheese custard. Bake in a moderate oven for about 30 minutes. Serve hot or cold with a green salad.
To freeze: Open freeze in flan ring, then remove from tin, wrap in aluminium foil, label and freeze. Re-heat from frozen at 190°C, 375°F, Gas Mark 5, for 40–50 minutes.

Spinach soufflé

Metric	*Imperial*
155g frozen leaf spinach	*5½oz frozen leaf spinach*
Knob of butter	*Knob of butter*
½ onion, peeled and finely chopped	*½ onion, peeled and finely chopped*
Salt and freshly ground black pepper	*Salt and freshly ground black pepper*
40g butter	*1½oz butter*
25g plain flour	*1oz plain flour*
150ml milk	*¼ pint milk*
3 eggs, separated	*3 eggs, separated*
½ teaspoon dried thyme	*½ teaspoon dried thyme*
25g Cheddar cheese, finely grated	*1oz Cheddar cheese, finely grated*

Cooking Time: 45–50 minutes
Oven: 180°C, 350°F, Gas Mark 4

Grease a 15cm (6in) soufflé dish. Heat the frozen spinach over a low heat and add a knob of butter. Stir in the onion and season well. Melt butter in another pan and add flour. Cook for a few minutes. Allow to cool slightly before adding the milk gradually. Bring to the boil, stirring, until sauce thickens. Cook for a further 3 minutes. Allow to cool, then add the egg yolks, beating in well. Stir in thyme and cheese. Put 2 × 15ml spoons (2 tablespoons) of the sauce into the spinach mixture, then pour this into the base of the soufflé dish. Whisk up the egg whites until just holding their shape. Fold these into the white sauce using a metal spoon. Pour this over the spinach. Bake in a moderate oven for about 45–50 minutes until risen and golden brown. Serve immediately with a tomato and onion salad.

Kipper and cheese flan; Bacon and egg pie; Spinach soufflé

Quick tuna pizza

Metric	Imperial
40g margarine	1½oz margarine
175g self-raising flour	6oz self-raising flour
1 × 5ml spoon salt	1 teaspoon salt
3–4 × 15ml spoons milk	3–4 tablespoons milk
25g margarine	1oz margarine
1 onion, peeled and sliced	1 onion, peeled and sliced
198g can tuna fish, drained and mashed	7oz can tuna fish, drained and mashed
1 × 5ml spoon dried basil	1 teaspoon dried basil
100g Cheddar cheese, finely grated	4oz Cheddar cheese, finely grated
2 tomatoes, sliced	2 tomatoes, sliced

Cooking Time: 20 minutes
Oven: 220°C, 425°F, Gas Mark 7

For the scone dough base rub fat into flour and salt. Bind together with milk. Roll lightly to a 20cm (8in) round and place on a greased baking tray. Heat margarine and fry onion until soft. Spread over scone base. Top onions with tuna fish. Mix herbs and cheese together and sprinkle over the fish. Top with tomato slices and bake in a hot oven for 15–20 minutes. Serve hot in wedges.

Courgettes with tomatoes and herbs

Metric	Imperial
450g courgettes, washed and thickly sliced	1lb courgettes, washed and thickly sliced
25g butter	1oz butter
4 tomatoes, peeled and roughly chopped	4 tomatoes, peeled and roughly chopped
1 clove of garlic, peeled and crushed	1 clove of garlic, peeled and crushed
1 × 15ml spoon chopped parsley	1 tablespoon chopped parsley
1 × 5ml spoon dried thyme	1 teaspoon dried thyme
Salt and freshly ground black pepper	Salt and freshly ground black pepper
50g Cheddar cheese, finely grated	2oz Cheddar cheese, finely grated
15g fresh white breadcrumbs	½oz fresh white breadcrumbs

Cooking Time: 20–25 minutes
Oven: 180°C, 350°F, Gas Mark 4

Bring the courgettes to the boil in salted water and cook for 3 minutes. Drain and place in an ovenproof dish. Heat butter, add tomatoes, garlic, parsley, thyme, seasoning, and cook until a thickish mixture forms. Taste and adjust seasoning and spoon over courgettes. Sprinkle with cheese and breadcrumbs. Bake in a moderate oven for about 20–25 minutes. Serve hot by itself, or with beefburgers, chops or steaks.

Tomato stuffed pancakes

Metric	Imperial
For the batter:	For the batter:
100g plain flour, sieved	4oz plain flour, sieved
¼ teaspoon salt	¼ teaspoon salt
1 egg, beaten	1 egg, beaten
300ml milk	½ pint milk
Oil for frying pancakes	Oil for frying pancakes
For the sauce:	For the sauce:
25g butter	1oz butter
½ onion, peeled and finely chopped	½ onion, peeled and finely chopped
4 tomatoes, peeled and roughly chopped	4 tomatoes, peeled and roughly chopped
100g mushrooms, washed and chopped	4oz mushrooms, washed and chopped
1 × 5ml spoon mixed herbs	1 teaspoon mixed herbs
25g fresh white breadcrumbs	1oz fresh white breadcrumbs
Salt and freshly ground black pepper	Salt and freshly ground black pepper
75g Cheddar cheese, grated	3oz Cheddar cheese, grated
300ml white coating sauce	½ pint white coating sauce

Cooking Time: 30 minutes
Oven: 190°C, 375°F, Gas Mark 5

Put flour and salt in a bowl. Add beaten egg and half the milk. Beat until smooth. Stir in the rest of the milk. Make 8 pancakes using the batter mixture. Heat butter and fry onion, tomatoes and mushrooms until reduced to a pulp. Stir in herbs, breadcrumbs, and season well. Divide the mixture between the pancakes, roll them up and place them in an ovenproof dish. Stir 50g (2oz) cheese into the white sauce, season and pour over the pancakes. Sprinkle over the remaining cheese and cook in a moderately hot oven for 30 minutes. Serve with a tossed green salad.

Quick tuna pizza; Tomato stuffed pancakes; Courgettes with tomatoes and herbs

Tuna fish pâté

Metric	Imperial
2 × 198g cans tuna fish, drained	2 × 7oz cans tuna fish, drained
50g butter, melted	2oz butter, melted
1 × 15ml spoon olive oil	1 tablespoon olive oil
Juice and finely grated rind of ½ lemon	Juice and finely grated rind of ½ lemon
25g fresh white breadcrumbs	1oz fresh white breadcrumbs
Salt and freshly ground black pepper	Salt and freshly ground black pepper
To finish:	To finish:
Lemon wedges	Lemon wedges
Parsley sprigs	Parsley sprigs

Cut tuna into small pieces and place mixture in a blender goblet with butter and oil. Blend until smooth. Turn into a bowl and stir in the lemon rind and juice, and breadcrumbs. Mix well and add plenty of seasoning. Spoon into a serving dish and garnish with lemon wedges and a sprig of parsley. Serve with toast.

To freeze: Cover pâté with foil, label and freeze. Thaw for 6 hours in the refrigerator.

Haddock and cheese mousse

Metric	Imperial
225g fresh haddock fillet	8oz fresh haddock fillet
75g cream cheese	3oz cream cheese
1 × 15ml spoon juice and finely grated rind of ½ lemon	1 tablespoon juice and finely grated rind of ½ lemon
Freshly ground black pepper	Freshly ground black pepper
To finish:	To finish:
Lemon slices	Lemon slices
Parsley sprigs	Parsley sprigs

This is quick to prepare and tastes delicious. It is ideal for quick snacks and picnics. Poach haddock fillet for 5–10 minutes. Drain, remove skin and flake fish. Beat cream cheese with lemon juice and rind. Season with freshly ground black pepper and add flaked fish. Beat well together and spoon into a serving dish. Garnish with lemon twists and parsley sprigs. Serve with toast or crackers.

Quick chicken liver pâté

Metric	Imperial
75g butter	3oz butter
1 medium-sized onion, peeled and chopped	1 medium-sized onion, peeled and chopped
225g chicken livers, trimmed and cut in halves	8oz chicken livers, trimmed and cut in halves
½ teaspoon dried thyme	½ teaspoon dried thyme
1 clove of garlic, peeled and crushed	1 clove of garlic, peeled and crushed
Salt and freshly ground black pepper	Salt and freshly ground black pepper
1 bay leaf	1 bay leaf
2 × 5ml spoons medium dry sherry or brandy (optional)	2 teaspoons medium dry sherry or brandy (optional)
To finish:	To finish:
75g butter, melted	3oz butter, melted
Parsley sprigs	Parsley sprigs

Heat butter and fry onions for a few minutes. Add the chicken livers, thyme, garlic, seasoning and bay leaf and cook until livers are just brown – about 5 minutes. Allow to cool slightly, remove bay leaf. Chop finely or pour into a blender goblet. Add sherry or brandy, purée to a cream and spoon into 4 individual dishes or 1 large dish. Place in the refrigerator to harden.

To finish: Pour a little melted butter over each and garnish with a sprig of parsley. Serve with toast or French bread.

Haddock and cheese mousse; Tuna fish pâté; Quick chicken liver pâté

Pork and liver pie

Metric	Imperial
275g plain flour	10oz plain flour
1 × 5ml spoon salt	1 teaspoon salt
4 × 15ml spoons cold water	4 tablespoons cold water
125g butter, softened	5oz butter, softened
1 egg, beaten	1 egg, beaten
325g pig's liver, ducts removed, and minced	12oz pig's liver, ducts removed, and minced
1 small onion, peeled and minced	1 small onion, peeled and minced
1 clove of garlic, peeled and crushed	1 clove of garlic, peeled and crushed
325g pork sausage meat	12oz pork sausage meat
Salt and freshly ground black pepper	Salt and freshly ground black pepper
1 egg, hard-boiled and chopped	1 egg, hard-boiled and chopped
1–2 × 5ml spoons dried thyme	1–2 teaspoons dried thyme
450g minced pork (or chicken)	1lb minced pork (or chicken)
3 rashers streaky bacon, rinded and minced	3 rashers streaky bacon, rinded and minced
Beaten egg for glazing	Beaten egg for glazing

Cooking Time: 1½ hours
Oven: 200°C, 400°F, Gas Mark 6
Reduce to: 180°C, 350°F, Gas Mark 4

This is not difficult to prepare and a marvellous way to use left-over meats with freshly bought meat. It is ideal for a picnic. Put flour in a bowl, dissolve salt in the water, add the butter, beaten egg and salt water to the flour. Knead the ingredients well together until smooth. Wrap in a plastic bag and leave in the refrigerator while preparing the filling. Combine the liver, onion, garlic and sausage meat together. Season well and stir in the chopped egg and herbs. In another bowl mix the pork and bacon together and season well. Line a 15cm (6in) round cake tin with three-quarters of the pastry. Spoon the liver mixture over the base, top with the pork and bacon mixture. Roll out the remaining pastry and cover the pie, sealing the edges well with beaten egg. Trim pastry and flute edges. Make a pastry tassel using left-overs, brush pastry with egg and bake in a hot oven for 30 minutes. Reduce oven temperature, cover pie with foil and cook for a further hour. Allow to cool in the tin, remove and serve cold with salads.

To make a pastry tassel: Roll out a strip of pastry to 10cm × 2½cm (4in × 1in). Make 1cm (¼in) cuts along the length to within 1cm (¼in) of the edge. Roll strip up, secure edges with water. Place completed tassel in the centre of the pie

Scotch eggs

Metric	Imperial
4 eggs, hard-boiled	4 eggs, hard-boiled
25g seasoned flour	1oz seasoned flour
225g pork sausage meat	8oz pork sausage meat
1 beaten egg	1 beaten egg
Breadcrumbs for coating	Breadcrumbs for coating
Oil for deep frying	Oil for deep frying

Cooking Time: 8 minutes

Toss eggs in seasoned flour. Divide sausage meat into 4 and roll each piece into a circle, large enough to surround the egg, on a floured board. Place the eggs in the centre of each circle and pinch the edges well together. Toss in egg and breadcrumbs. Deep fry in oil, heated to a temperature of 170°C, 340°F, for about 8 minutes until crisp and lightly browned. Drain on kitchen paper. Serve hot or cold with a green salad.

Sandwiches

Sandwich Fillings:
1) Canned salmon, mashed with mayonnaise and topped with cucumber slices.
2) Chopped tongue, mayonnaise, pinch curry powder, chopped spring onions.
3) Mashed sardines, black pepper and lemon juice.
4) Cream cheese and chopped celery.
5) Mashed bananas and honey.

Toasted Sandwiches: Butter two pieces of toast and fill with one of the following fillings:
1) 2 bacon rashers, rinded and grilled and topped with 50g (2oz) grated cheese and grilled until cheese melts.
2) 1 tomato, sliced and topped with a slice of gruyère cheese and grilled until cheese melts.
3) Mix baked beans with dry mustard and spread over toast. Top with crumbled cooked bacon.

Scotch eggs; Sandwiches; Pork and liver pie

All-in-one chocolate cake

Metric

125g soft margarine
125g caster sugar
2 large eggs
1 × 15ml spoon milk
125g self-raising flour
25g cocoa powder
1 × 5ml spoon baking
powder
100g butter, softened
225g icing sugar, sieved
1 × 15ml spoon milk
Finely grated rind of 1
orange

To finish:
125g dark cooking
chocolate, broken into
pieces
25g butter

Imperial

4oz soft margarine
4oz caster sugar
2 large eggs
1 tablespoon milk
4oz self-raising flour
1oz cocoa powder
1 teaspoon baking
powder
4oz butter, softened
8oz icing sugar, sieved
1 tablespoon milk
Finely grated rind of 1
orange

To finish:
4oz dark cooking
chocolate, broken into
pieces
1oz butter

Cooking Time: 35 minutes
Oven: 170°C, 325°F, Gas Mark 3

Grease two 18cm (7in) sandwich tins and line bases with greased greaseproof paper. Place margarine, caster sugar, eggs, milk, flour, cocoa powder and baking powder in a bowl. Beat for 3–4 minutes. Divide the mixture between the tins and bake in a warm oven for 30–35 minutes until cakes spring back when lightly pressed. Leave in tins for 2 minutes then turn out onto a wire rack and remove the greaseproof paper. Leave to cool.

For butter icing place the softened butter in a bowl and beat to a cream. Gradually beat in the icing sugar alternately with the milk and continue beating until light and fluffy. Stir in the grated orange rind.

To finish: When cakes are cold sandwich layers together with the butter icing. Melt the chocolate in a bowl over a pan of hot water. Remove from the heat and beat in butter. When of spreading consistency, spread chocolate topping over top of cake.

All-in-one chocolate cake

Cherry and almond topped cake

Metric

225g soft margarine
225g caster sugar
4 large eggs
225g plain flour
½ teaspoon powdered cinnamon
½ teaspoon powdered mace
450g currants, sultanas, raisins, mixed together
75g glacé cherries, quartered
50g mixed peel

Topping:
50g glacé cherries, quartered
50g mixed peel
25g flaked almonds

Imperial

8oz soft margarine
8oz caster sugar
4 large eggs
8oz plain flour
½ teaspoon powdered cinnamon
½ teaspoon powdered mace
1lb currants, sultanas, raisins, mixed together
3oz glacé cherries, quartered
2oz mixed peel

Topping:
2oz glacé cherries, quartered
2oz mixed peel
1oz flaked almonds

Cooking Time: 2½–3 hours
Oven: 150°C, 300°F, Gas Mark 2

Grease and line a 20cm (8in) cake tin, with oiled greaseproof paper. Cream margarine and sugar together for 2 minutes if using an electric beater, or for 4–5 minutes if using a wooden spoon. Beat eggs into mixture. Stir in the sieved flour and spices and finally the fruit. Spoon mixture into the prepared tin.
For the topping: Mix together the cherries, mixed peel and almonds, and sprinkle over the surface of the cake. Cook in a slow oven for about 2½ hours. Allow to cool slightly in the tin before turning out.

Cherry and almond topped cake

Christmas cake

Metric	Imperial
175g currants	6oz currants
225g stoned raisins, chopped	8oz stoned raisins, chopped
225g sultanas	8oz sultanas
100g glacé cherries, halved	4oz glacé cherries, halved
100g mixed peel	4oz mixed peel
50g angelica, chopped	2oz angelica, chopped
50g chopped almonds	2oz chopped almonds
Finely grated rind of 1 lemon	Finely grated rind of 1 lemon
225g plain flour	8oz plain flour
1 × 5ml spoon mixed spice	1 teaspoon mixed spice
225g butter, softened	8oz butter, softened
225g soft brown sugar	8oz soft brown sugar
1 × 15ml spoon black treacle	1 tablespoon black treacle
4 large eggs	4 large eggs
1–2 × 15ml spoons brandy or sherry	1–2 tablespoons brandy or sherry

Cooking Time: 3½–4 hours
Oven: 150°C, 300°F, Gas Mark 2

Grease and line a 20cm (8in) round cake tin. Tie newspaper or brown paper band around the tin. Put all the dried fruit in a bowl. Stir in the nuts and lemon rind. Sieve the flour and spice together. Cream the butter, sugar and treacle together until light and fluffy. Beat in the eggs, stir in the sieved flour and spices. Finally stir in the mixed fruit and mix thoroughly. Turn into the tin and make a slight hollow in the centre. Bake in a slow oven for 3½–4 hours. Cool in the tin before turning out on a wire rack to cool completely. Prick the surface of the cake all over with a fine skewer and pour over brandy or sherry before storing.

To ice: Almond paste the cake first using 675g (1½lb) ready-made almond paste. Allow a few days for this to harden before applying the icing. Make royal icing using 3 egg whites and ¾kg (1½lb icing sugar and 2 × 5ml spoons (2 teaspoons) glycerine. Rough ice the cake and use bought decorations to decorate.

Continental apple

Metric	Imperial
For the topping:	For the topping:
25g butter	1oz butter
75g self-raising flour	3oz self-raising flour
25g caster sugar	1oz caster sugar
1 × 15ml spoon water	1 tablespoon water
For the base:	For the base:
50g margarine	2oz margarine
50g caster sugar	2oz caster sugar
1 large egg, beaten	1 large egg, beaten
Few drops vanilla essence	Few drops vanilla essence
100g self-raising flour	4oz self-raising flour
2 medium-sized cooking apples, peeled, cored and sliced	2 medium-sized cooking apples, peeled, cored and sliced
To finish:	To finish:
1 red eating apple, sliced	1 red eating apple, sliced

Cooking Time: 1 hour
Oven: 180°C, 350°F, Gas Mark 4

This would be equally delicious served as a pudding. Grease a 20cm (8in) sandwich tin and line base with non-stick paper. For the topping rub butter into flour and stir in sugar. Sprinkle on water and mix until the mixture becomes lumpy. Leave on one side. Cream margarine and sugar together until light and fluffy, beat in egg and vanilla essence and finally stir in flour. Spread this across the base of the prepared tin, arrange drained apple slices on top and finally sprinkle crumble topping over apple to cover completely. Cook in a moderate oven for about 1 hour. Cool slightly before turning out. Decorate with apple slices, serve with whipped cream.

Gingerbread

Metric	Imperial
225g plain flour	8oz plain flour
Pinch salt	Pinch salt
3 × 5ml spoons ground ginger	3 teaspoons ground ginger
100g butter or margarine	4oz butter or margarine
40g soft brown sugar	1½oz soft brown sugar
100g golden syrup	4oz golden syrup
100g black treacle	4oz black treacle
1 × 5ml spoon bicarbonate of soda	1 teaspoon bicarbonate of soda
1 egg, beaten	1 egg, beaten
300ml warm milk	½ pint warm milk

Cooking Time: 1¼ hours
Oven: 170°C, 350°F, Gas Mark 4

Grease and line the base of a 17cm (7 in) square cake tin, with greaseproof paper. Sieve the flour, salt and ginger in a bowl. Gently heat the butter, brown sugar, syrup and treacle in a pan until the fat melts. Sprinkle the bicarbonate of soda into the warmed milk. Gradually beat the melted butter and treacle mixture into the dry ingredients until smooth. Finally beat in the egg and milk. Pour into the prepared tin and cook in a moderate oven for about 1¼ hours. Cool slightly in the tin before turning out on a wire rack. Store in foil or an airtight tin. Serve in slices, plain or buttered.

Continental apple; Christmas cake; Gingerbread

Scones – sweet and cheese

Metric

50g butter
225g self-raising flour
25g caster sugar
40g dried fruit or
50g Cheddar cheese,
finely grated
150ml milk

To finish:
Milk to glaze
Sugar for sprinkling, or
Grated cheese for
sprinkling

Imperial

2oz butter
8oz self-raising flour
1oz caster sugar
1½oz dried fruit, or
2oz Cheddar cheese,
finely grated
¼ pint milk

To finish:
Milk to glaze
Sugar for sprinkling, or
Grated cheese for
sprinkling

Cooking Time: 8–10 minutes
Oven: 220°C, 425°F, Gas Mark 7

Rub the fat into the flour. Stir in the sugar, fruit or cheese. Pour in the milk and mix lightly with a knife to a firm, slightly sticky dough. Toss lightly in flour and shape or roll into a round, about 1cm (½in) thick. Cut into rounds using a 5cm (2in) fluted cutter for sweet scones and a plain one for cheese. Place on a greased baking sheet, brush tops with milk and sprinkle lightly with sugar or cheese. Cook near the top of a hot oven for about 8–10 minutes. Allow to cool slightly, halve and serve buttered.
Makes approx 8–10

Welsh girdle cakes

Metric

225g plain flour
½ teaspoon baking powder
½ teaspoon mixed spice
50g margarine
50g lard
75g currants
50–75g sugar
1 standard egg
1 × 15ml spoon milk

To finish:
Extra sugar for sprinkling

Imperial

8oz plain flour
½ teaspoon baking powder
½ teaspoon mixed spice
2oz margarine
2oz lard
3oz currants
2–3oz sugar
1 standard egg
1 tablespoon milk

To finish:
Extra sugar for sprinkling

Cooking Time: 15 minutes

These cakes are ideal for children's teas and to take on picnics, as they store well in an airtight container. Sieve flour with baking powder and mixed spice. Rub fats into flour. Add currants and sugar and mix well together with the egg and milk to form a stiff paste. Roll out on a lightly floured board to about 6mm (¼in) thick. Cut into rounds using a 5cm (2in) fluted cutter. Bake on a girdle over medium heat until lightly brown on each side. When cool, sprinkle with extra sugar.
Makes 24

Wholemeal soda bread

Metric

225g plain flour
1 × 5ml bicarbonate of
soda
2 × 5ml spoons cream of
   tartar
1 × 5ml spoon salt
225g plain wholemeal
flour
25g margarine
300ml milk
Flour for sprinkling

Imperial

8oz plain flour
1 teaspoon bicarbonate
of soda
2 teaspoons cream of
   tartar
1 teaspoon salt
8oz plain wholemeal
flour
1oz margarine
½ pint milk
Flour for sprinkling

Cooking Time: 35 minutes
Oven: 200°C, 400°F, Gas Mark 6

Sieve the white flour, bicarbonate of soda, cream of tartar and salt in a bowl. Stir in the wholemeal flour. Rub in the margarine. Bind together with milk to form a soft dough. Knead on a floured board, shape into 1 large or 2 small rounds, place on a greased baking sheet, score the surface and sprinkle with flour. Bake in a hot oven for 35 minutes. This bread should be eaten on the day it is made.

Scones – sweet and cheese; Wholemeal soda bread; Welsh girdle cakes; Crispy crackles

Crispy crackles

Metric	Imperial
50g butter	*2oz butter*
2 × 15ml spoons golden syrup	*2 tablespoons golden syrup*
50g drinking chocolate, sifted	*2oz drinking chocolate, sifted*
50g cornflakes	*2oz cornflakes*

Cooking Time: 3 minutes

These are always a popular favourite with children and quick and easy to make. Melt the butter and golden syrup over a low heat. Remove from the heat and stir in the drinking chocolate and cornflakes and mix well so the cornflakes are well coated in the chocolate syrup mixture. Spoon into paper cases, set on a baking sheet and leave to cool. They will set on cooling.

Makes 16

Chocolate fruit bars

Metric

90g butter
1 × 15ml spoon golden
syrup
225g muesli
25g stoned raisins,
chopped
50g glacé cherries, finely
chopped
25g angelica, chopped
100g plain chocolate

Imperial

3½oz butter
1 tablespoon golden
syrup
8oz muesli
1oz stoned raisins,
chopped
2oz glacé cherries, finely
chopped
1oz angelica, chopped
4oz plain chocolate

These are un-baked so are quick to make and ideal for picnics or packed lunches. Melt butter and add syrup. Remove from heat and stir in muesli, raisins, cherries and angelica. Press into a greased 17cm (7in) square shallow cake tin. Melt chocolate in a basin over a pan of hot water, spread over mixture in tin and mark with a fork. Chill and cut into bars.

Makes 12

Shortbread biscuits

Metric

175g plain flour
Good pinch of salt
125g butter, softened
40g caster sugar
Extra sugar for sprinkling

Imperial

6oz plain flour
Good pinch of salt
4oz butter, softened
1½oz caster sugar
Extra sugar for sprinkling

Cooking Time: 20 minutes
Oven: 170°C, 325°F, Gas Mark 3

Place the flour in a bowl with the salt. Add the butter and sugar and knead mixture into a ball. Turn onto a lightly floured board and shape into a round. Flour the rolling pin and roll the mixture out to about 1cm (½in) thick. Using a 6cm (2½in) fluted cutter, cut into rounds and place on a baking sheet. Sprinkle lightly with sugar and cook in a warm oven for about 15–20 minutes.

Makes 12–16 biscuits

Piped biscuits

Metric

100g soft margarine
25g icing sugar, sieved
75g plain flour
25g cornflour
Few drops of vanilla
essence
Glacé cherries and
angelica for decoration

Imperial

4oz soft margarine
1oz icing sugar, sieved
3oz plain flour
1oz cornflour
Few drops of vanilla
essence
Glacé cherries and
angelica for decoration

Cooking Time: 10 minutes
Oven: 190°C, 375°F, Gas Mark 5

Line a baking sheet with non-stick paper. Cream the margarine and icing sugar together until smooth. Stir in the flour and cornflour with the vanilla essence. Spoon the mixture into a piping bag fitted with a 1cm (½in) star vegetable nozzle. Pipe the mixture in different shapes, i.e. stars, whirls and fingers, onto the lined baking sheet. Decorate with pieces of glacé cherries and angelica. Bake in a moderately hot oven for about 8–10 minutes. Cool on a wire rack.

Makes 16–18 biscuits

Shortbread biscuits; Piped biscuits; Chocolate fruit bars; Redcurrant and almond tartlets

Redcurrant and almond tartlets

Metric

Shortcrust pastry made with 175g plain flour, 100g fat, and 2 × 15ml spoons cold water
3 × 15ml spoons redcurrant jelly
40g soft margarine
50g caster sugar
1 standard egg
25g self-raising flour
50g ground almonds

Imperial

Shortcrust pastry made with 6oz plain flour, 4oz fat, and 2 tablespoons cold water
3 tablespoons redcurrant jelly
1½oz soft margarine
2oz caster sugar
1 standard egg
1oz self-raising flour
2oz ground almonds

Cooking Time: 15 minutes
Oven: 200°C, 400°F, Gas Mark 6

Line 18 patty tins with the thinly rolled pastry. Spoon a little redcurrant jelly into the base of each pastry case. Cream the margarine and sugar together until light and fluffy. Beat in the egg, stir in the flour and almonds. Divide this mixture between the pastry cases. Bake in a hot oven for about 15 minutes. Cool on a wire rack.
Makes 18

Index